Inclusive Territories 2

Territorial Entrepreneurship
and Innovation Set
coordinated by
Didier Chabaud, Florent Pratlong
and Carlos Moreno

Volume 2

Inclusive Territories 2

Role of Institutions and Local Actors

Edited by

Martine Brasseur
Annie Bartoli
Didier Chabaud
Pascal Grouiez
Gilles Rouet

WILEY

First published 2024 in Great Britain and the United States by ISTE Ltd and John Wiley & Sons, Inc.

Apart from any fair dealing for the purposes of research or private study, or criticism or review, as permitted under the Copyright, Designs and Patents Act 1988, this publication may only be reproduced, stored or transmitted, in any form or by any means, with the prior permission in writing of the publishers, or in the case of reprographic reproduction in accordance with the terms and licenses issued by the CLA. Enquiries concerning reproduction outside these terms should be sent to the publishers at the undermentioned address:

ISTE Ltd
27-37 St George's Road
London SW19 4EU
UK

www.iste.co.uk

John Wiley & Sons, Inc.
111 River Street
Hoboken, NJ 07030
USA

www.wiley.com

© ISTE Ltd 2024

The rights of Martine Brasseur, Annie Bartoli, Didier Chabaud, Pascal Grouiez and Gilles Rouet to be identified as the authors of this work have been asserted them in accordance with the Copyright, Designs and Patents Act 1988.

Any opinions, findings, and conclusions or recommendations expressed in this material are those of the author(s), contributor(s) or editor(s) and do not necessarily reflect the views of ISTE Group.

Library of Congress Control Number: 2023945011

British Library Cataloguing-in-Publication Data
A CIP record for this book is available from the British Library
ISBN 978-1-78630-856-6

Contents

Introduction xi
Annie BARTOLI, Martine BRASSEUR and Gilles ROUET

Part 1. Inclusion of Discriminated and Marginalized Populations in a Territory

Chapter 1. The Inclusion of People from Disadvantaged Territories: Two SMEs in Seine-Saint-Denis. 3
Hacène LAÏCHOUR, Jean-François CHANLAT and Jean-Marie PERETTI

    1.1. Corporate social responsibility (CSR) policies and diversity
in SMEs. 4
        1.1.1. Diversity and social responsibility 4
        1.1.2. Diversity and territorial responsibility. 5
    1.2. Barriers and drivers for the recruitment and integration of people
from disadvantaged areas 6
        1.2.1. Recruitment 8
        1.2.2. Integration 9
    1.3. Contextualizing the inclusion of people from disadvantaged
territories. 14
        1.3.1. Supporting urban recruitment through SMEs 14
        1.3.2. Difficulties of employee inclusion 15
    1.4. Conclusion 17
    1.5. References 17

Chapter 2. "Territories with Zero Long-Term Unemployment" through the Lens of Neo-Institutional Theory. 21
Amina SAYDI and Martine BRASSEUR

    2.1. Inclusive practice 22

2.1.1. Inclusion 22
2.1.2. The social enterprise 23
2.2. The perspective of neo-institutional theory 24
    2.2.1. The institution as a product of actors 25
    2.2.2. Actors initiating change 26
    2.2.3. The contributions of neo-institutional theory to the question
    of the diffusion of inclusive practices. 28
2.3. Case study: the territories with zero long-term unemployment
experiment 30
    2.3.1. A collective approach for another way to achieve
    entrepreneurship 30
    2.3.2. An experiment in search of diffusion 32
    2.3.3. A program in search of legitimacy. 34
2.4. Conclusion 35
2.5. References 36

**Chapter 3. The Inclusion of Lebanese Women with Breast
Cancer: Between Stigma and Resilience** 41
Nathalie CARIOU GHANTOUS, Jean-François CHANLAT and
Laurence FROLOFF BROUCHE

3.1. From a social identity robbed by disease to stigmatization and
resilience 42
3.2. The perspectives of 25 Lebanese women with breast cancer in
the workplace 45
    3.2.1. Beginning of the disease cycle and its representation in
    companies 45
    3.2.2. Work cycle, illness cycle: concordances 47
    3.2.3. Resilience and trajectories. 50
3.3. Conclusion 52
3.4. References 53

**Chapter 4. Women Entrepreneurs from Deprived Areas as
Generators of Inclusion: A Capabilities Interpretation.** 57
Amélie NOTAIS and Julie TIXIER

4.1. Proposition of a framework for analyzing the inclusive territory 58
    4.1.1. Inclusive territory: a fuzzy target. 58
    4.1.2. Generating inclusion: from concept to action 59
4.2. A qualitative and sensitive approach to local women's
entrepreneurship. 61
4.3. The capabilities of women entrepreneurs: a potential tool for
inclusion 64
    4.3.1. Environmental conversion factors 64

4.3.2. Social conversion factors 65
4.3.3. Individual conversion factors. 67
4.4. The contribution of capabilities and the question of granularity 68
4.5. Conclusion 70
4.6. References 70

Part 2. The Stakeholders of Inclusive Entrepreneurial Ecosystems

Chapter 5. From Fighting Exclusion to Projects for Inclusion: The Evolution of Public and Private Policies 75
Annie BARTOLI and Gilles ROUET

5.1. A brief history of the fight against social exclusion in France 76
   5.1.1. Exclusion as a sign of social maladjustment that can be overcome by employment and the economy. 77
   5.1.2. Citizen solidarity: combating the cultural dimension of social exclusion. 77
   5.1.3. Market exclusion: an indicator of long-term unemployment questioning social rights. 79
   5.1.4. Exclusion as a process of disaffiliation and vulnerability combated by social and family support. 80
   5.1.5. Exclusion as a marker of marginality or even of refusal of assistance 80
   5.1.6. A case-by-case approach to combating social exclusion and individual disintegration. 81
   5.1.7. Social exclusion: an inevitable dysfunction of modern society . . . 82
   5.1.8. From the fight against exclusion to inclusion projects: beyond a simple mirroring of reasoning 84
5.2. European policies: from anti-exclusion to pro-inclusion incentives. 85
   5.2.1. Community policies to combat social exclusion. 85
   5.2.2. Towards an EU-wide approach to inclusion 86
5.3. Corporate dynamics and inclusive policies 88
   5.3.1. Inclusion as a CSR variable. 89
   5.3.2. "Diversity and inclusion": the new managerial policies of large multinational companies 90
5.4. Public policies for inclusion at the territorial level. 96
   5.4.1. The development of the "inclusive city" 97
   5.4.2. Towards a societal role for local authorities 98
5.5. Conclusion 100
5.6. References 101

Chapter 6. Inclusive Governance in AOC Champagne. 105
Mathilde CHOMLAFEL and Jean-Paul MÉREAUX

6.1. The Champagne sector as a practice area for the implementation
of inclusive governance 107
   6.1.1. A history of the relations between the actors of the
champagne production chain 107
   6.1.2. The Champagne region as a constructed space, bearing
identities 109
   6.1.3. Exclusion as a fertile ground for inclusion in the territory
of AOC Champagne 111
   6.1.4. Promoting inclusion to ensure the sustainability of the
Champagne sector 113
6.2. A literature review of professional perspectives in the context
of the Covid-19 pandemic 115
6.3. Inclusive governance in AOC Champagne 121
6.4. Conclusion 123
6.5. References 124

Chapter 7. Promoting Inclusive Partnership Dynamics within a Territory: The Case of Territories with Zero Long-Term Unemployment 127
Jean-Christophe SARROT

7.1. The impotence of public policies in the face of unemployment
in France 128
7.2. Building a new common good: employment 129
7.3. A source as close as possible to the territories 130
7.4. Unprecedented unanimity in the French Parliament 131
7.5. Confidence in the unemployed (an excluded population) 132
7.6. The local employment committee: a new tool for shared
governance 134
7.7. The role of the actors' representations 136
7.8. Compensation for territorial inequalities 137
7.9. Changing attitudes 137
7.10. An unprecedented articulation between the territory and the
national dimension 138
7.11. Social work transformed by access to employment for all 140
7.12. Highlighting the different aspects of poverty 141
7.13. New indicators to move towards an "unknown desirable" 141
7.14. Conclusion 142
7.15. References 143

Chapter 8. The Contribution of Quebec's Community Credit Organizations to Social and Territorial Development 145
Marie LANGEVIN and Annie-Claude VEILLEUX

    8.1. Community credit in Quebec 147
    8.2. Community credit and inclusive dynamics in the territories:
    the Mauricie region. 151
        8.2.1. The socio-economic profile of the Mauricie region. 151
        8.2.2. Proximity support and the creation and maintenance of
        businesses and jobs. 154
        8.2.3. Factors of social inclusion: atypical entrepreneurs 156
        8.2.4. The entrepreneurial ecosystem: diversification and
        networking. 159
        8.2.5. The community's contribution to the community 162
    8.3. Conclusion 163
    8.4. References 164

Conclusion. 167
Martine BRASSEUR

List of Authors 173

Index 175

Introduction

Local Ecosystems that Undertake to Promote Inclusion

Since 2020, the Covid-19 pandemic has led to a new awareness of "territories", which have often been blamed for the globalization and financialization of the economy or obscured by these processes. In the 21st century, territories appear to be at the center of various societal concerns, and are considered to be relevant spaces regarding the increasingly sought-after balance between the global and local spheres. They can be analyzed as places of sociability, identification, individual or collective anchoring and even solidarity. Territorialization, or a need for territory, is a crucial part of individuals' daily lives. However, it is also essential for companies and organizations more generally and can provide a framework to their stakeholders who need it. The topic of territories cuts across geography, politics and economics, as well as sociology, anthropology and psychology, among other disciplines.

Territories are also thought of by way of digital technology, networks and interactions. They emerge then as a network in the virtual world that does not resemble local coordinations or physical neighborhoods. As such, the traditional approaches to territory in terms of distance or proximity have been called into question, since territories can no longer be defined solely according to geographical criteria. However, whether a territory is physical or virtual and whether the relations that are forged there are direct or digital, inclusion can be seen as an objective, a value and a dynamic.

Introduction written by Annie BARTOLI, Martine BRASSEUR and Gilles ROUET.

Territories are the subject of numerous planning processes and programs that aim to improve the daily lives of inhabitants. The areas of intervention are numerous – employment, the environment, transport and communication infrastructures, education, culture, health, etc. – and programs are targeted at categorizations of citizens, which change over time. Thus, sustainable changes can be made to contexts, urban or rural landscapes and uses linked to social or economic activities, as well as to various forms of consumption.

Investigations into citizens' expectations are increasingly being undertaken to support these approaches. In turn, the legitimacy of these approaches lies in their political project – whether on a local, regional or national scale, or even at the European or international level – as well as in their mediatization and the available resources that can be available to them. As for the concrete application of these numerous measures or perspectives, it is most often best left to the actors themselves, and in particular to the institutions and organizations within the territories concerned, even though the logics of these stakeholders are not all easily or spontaneously understood.

As far as companies in particular are concerned, although some of their actions can be attributed to economic and political factors or motivations, they have also developed a variety of inclusive approaches on their own behalf. Inclusion can therefore be defined as both a state and a process. Likewise, societies are experiencing a shift in the hierarchy of values, and it is no longer just a matter of putting in place mechanisms to combat exclusion; now, it is more a matter of advocating for the participation of organizations in a global social project that goes beyond social adjustments or systems for compensating inequalities and neglect.

At the heart of inclusive territorial dynamics, it is the actors, agents, citizens, users and organizations with their issues, interactions, implications, doubts and certainties, along with their contradictions, which together constitute elements of diversity, vitality or innovation. Inclusion in territories leads us to rethink the question of proximity, especially given the fact that relationships also exist through digital technology. Proximity, in its various forms, perhaps reflects an expectation that is linked to a search for meaning in action. Organizations have a de facto form of territorial responsibility, which is linked to the meaning attributed to their activities and the value generated. They are thus likely to be involved in cohesive approaches, responding to both internal and external expectations and promoting the creation or restoration of trust between social categories.

Organizations, and in particular companies, are thus important political actors with a role to play in sustainable development, social responsibility and inclusion. Alongside, or upstream of, these general considerations, numerous analyses and research perspectives make it possible to establish this global understanding in the current functioning of organizations: for example, the link between competitiveness and corporate social responsibility, the performance of relations between public contractors in an approach with societal stakes or the avoidance of relations between the company and the territory. However, territories are diverse, as are organizations and their modes of action, which are part of specific social and cultural realities. As such, a global theorization does not seem sufficient, as the analysis must take adaptations and contingencies into account.

Territorial development is, or should be, inclusive. In the past, certain policies have often centered around entrepreneurship, which creates activity and jobs, in order to revitalize regions, achieve reconversions or generate new social and economic opportunities. The entrepreneurial dynamics, in this global project of society, are therefore real instruments of territorialization, and hence of inclusion, not only because they can create jobs but also because they are meaningful for territories and for the coherence of the whole in terms of activities and implications for everyone.

This book, *Inclusive Territories 2*, follows a first volume that addressed inclusion on a territory as a project for organizations. This book is divided into two parts, which mirror our two angles of approach.

In Part 1, we focus on the initiatives that have been implemented in territories to support the inclusion of discriminated and excluded populations. In particular, we consider professional integration (Chapters 1 and 2) and equality and inequality between women and men (Chapters 3 and 4), which allow us to identify the ways in which SMEs (Chapter 1) and national programs (Chapter 2) – such as the territories with zero long-term unemployment scheme – contribute to promoting inclusion. The next two chapters deal with specific, but no less important, population groups that are discriminated against due to serious medical conditions (Chapter 3) or because of a person's place of origin or residence (Chapter 4).

Part 2 builds on this by examining the mobilization of all of the stakeholders in a territory. Chapter 5 puts public and private policies into perspective and attempts to show how we can move from attempting to combat exclusion towards a logic of inclusion project. The following chapters shed light on local mobilization mechanisms, focusing on the possibility of inclusive governance (Chapter 6) and the role of coordination instances (Chapter 7) and community credit organizations (Chapter 8).

In conclusion, this book leads to an analysis of the societal implications of inclusive dynamics in territories, regardless of their forms and modalities, while underlining the key role of organizations and the challenges for enterprises. It opens up an avenue of research that, while still little explored, is now unavoidable and concerns the decisive actions and conditions for the implementation of inclusive territorial processes.

PART 1

Inclusion of Discriminated and Marginalized Populations in a Territory

Part I

1

The Inclusion of People from Disadvantaged Territories: Two SMEs in Seine-Saint-Denis

The difficulties associated with the inclusion of people from disadvantaged French urban areas have attracted the attention of companies, particularly since the urban riots of 2005, and they have implemented dedicated managerial practices to tackle these challenges as part of their diversity and inclusion policies. However, the opposition of some managers to this approach has often led to the results being inconclusive. Although the inclusion of the people living in these urban areas (which suffer from a high unemployment rate regardless of age, gender and origin) is a major social and societal issue, there is still little research on the drivers and obstacles for the inclusion of people living in these areas (Labulle 2013; Mathivet and Raoul-Chassaing 2016; Jardat and Labulle 2018; Laïchour 2020).

However, this topic has been addressed in terms of the professional integration of people who struggle in terms of employment (Angotti et al. 2007; Cusin and Charreire-Petit 2015) and young people with low educational capital (Dufour 2008; Dufour and Lacaze 2010; Montargot 2013; Sabouné 2016). The issue of including populations from these urban territories presents not only important managerial issues because of the interest that this question may arouse among certain managers already more or less accustomed to recruiting in this employment pool, but also theoretical

---

Chapter written by Hacène LAÏCHOUR, Jean-François CHANLAT and Jean-Marie PERETTI.

ones by making it possible to better understand the existing dynamics of professional integration within these territories.

This research, which was conducted in two small- and medium-sized enterprises (SMEs) in these territories, focuses on inclusion, recruitment and integration on the basis that integration refers to a set of organizational practices implemented after the recruitment phase (Peretti 1994). The following research questions were formulated:

– What are the factors that led these companies to favor the recruitment of people from these areas and to do so without encountering much resistance?

– What practices were adopted to encourage their inclusion?

– Which employees did these practices apply to?

– What challenges have these companies faced in successfully fostering the inclusion of these employees?

1.1. Corporate social responsibility (CSR) policies and diversity in SMEs

In recent years, the management issue of diversity in the context of CSR (Chanlat et al. 2013) has progressively broadened to include SMEs and populations from disadvantaged territories (Labulle 2013; Mathivet and Raoul-Chassaing 2016; Jardat and Labulle 2018).

1.1.1. *Diversity and social responsibility*

Diversity management is clearly part of the social dimension of CSR (Bender and Pigeyre 2010) and aims to fight against all forms of discrimination, promote equal opportunities (Barth and Falcoz 2010) and foster inclusion (Barth 2018). In this framework, a company will adopt, whenever possible (Chanlat et al. 2013), specific managerial practices relating to professional support, diversity, identity recognition, social support and professional recognition, since the lack of such recognition at work can be linked to a high employee turnover rate (Dufour 2008). Companies will also implement communication actions so that the actors concerned do not perceive differences as a threat (Bruna et al. 2017). The factors influencing the adoption of a diversity approach are economic, legal, ethical and institutional, as well as external (e.g. location, sector of activity, history, etc.) and internal (e.g. management style, organizational culture, etc.) originating from within the company (Bruna et al. 2017; Chanlat and Özbilgin 2018, 2019).

If, within an SME, all of these factors are present, the managerial convictions of the director play an important role in the adoption of such an approach (Berger-Douce 2008, 2009; Igalens et al. 2011). These convictions are influenced by personality, social origin, personal experience and sensitivity to internal and external influences. The director of an SME, although they may also face opposition from certain organizational actors, nevertheless often enjoys greater flexibility to share their convictions and meet the expectations of these actors, particularly because of the size of the company and its proximity to its employees (Mahé de Boislandelle 1998; Naschberger and Guerfel-Henda 2013). SMEs are less likely to act on CSR issues when under pressure from civil society and are sometimes even able to distinguish themselves in this respect (Berger-Douce 2008, 2009). Some, due to a lack of financial resources or to enjoy greater visibility, join social organizations (federations, associations, etc.), and thus end up adopting identical practices. Regardless of the nature of its social commitment, an SME rarely puts it ahead of profit maximization (Paradas 2008; Bonneveux et al. 2011; Delchet-Cochet and Vo 2012; Bon et al. 2015).

1.1.2. *Diversity and territorial responsibility*

Managing diversity is also part of the societal dimension of CSR, particularly with regard to assessing a company's impact on the surrounding territory. For example, this can refer to the local jobs created by the company or to the nature of its relations with those affected by its activity, such as local associations or the populations of these disadvantaged territories (Duport et al. 2020).

French urban areas said to be disadvantaged were defined for the first time by law in 1996 and then redefined in 2014 under the name of priority neighborhoods for urban policy (*quartiers prioritaires de la politique de la ville* (QPVs)) (Darriau et al. 2014). They have been the subject of several measures at the urban (destruction/reconstruction of buildings, increase in the number of forms of transport, job creation in security, etc.), social (promoting success school, etc.) and economic (requiring, even financially encouraging, companies to recruit within these territories) levels (Conseil économique et social 2008). These territories, as well as those bordering them (Mathivet and Raoul-Chassaing 2016), face many problems: poor housing, a lack of transport services, high levels of insecurity, significant social homogeneity, high unemployment and poverty rates and a high number of immigrants, young people, low-skilled workers and struggling families, etc. (Darriau et al. 2014). In these areas, companies sometimes even have to make up for the shortcomings of the State (Dhaoudi 2008).

1.2. Barriers and drivers for the recruitment and integration of people from disadvantaged areas

Based on the obstacles and drivers that we identified in our literature review (Table 1.1), we conducted an empirical study that took the form of semi-structured interviews with 2 leaders of SMEs, 15 managers, 30 employees who were from disadvantaged urban areas and 3 who were not. Of the respondents, 60% were under 30 years of age and 26% were between 31 and 40 years of age; 73% had less than a baccalaureate (general or technological); 50% stated their North African or sub-Saharan origins; and 37% considered themselves to be French or from a country belonging to continental Europe. The respondents worked in two SMEs, one of which specialized in telecommunications and gas (company A), and the other in public works (company B). A and B were located in one of the disadvantaged urban areas of Seine-Saint-Denis and had committed themselves at an early stage to supporting the professional integration of young people, or less young people, from these areas.

The results of our empirical study show that managers – who were themselves influenced by the external environment of their respective companies – played an important, even decisive, role in recruitment and in the use of certain drivers for integration; there was a lack of resistance on the part of managers. On the other hand, some employees who had influence over some of the drivers did not always act in favor of the integration of this type of population.

	Recruitment of People from Disadvantaged Areas
Drivers	Economic: overcoming tensions specific to a sector of activity; promoting social exchanges with a type of clientele; carrying out an activity within these zones while avoiding reprisals against employees; reducing the distance between home and work; receiving state aid Legal: compliance with the law or with a social clause for professional integration Ethical: integration within a territory by way of socio-historical links; recognition of the local community Institutional: adherence to institutional mechanisms (signing of a charter, diversity training, participation in employment forums' sponsorship, etc.)
Obstacles	Economic discrimination: the negative reactions of customers; a type of population's productivity being perceived as inferior (Gobillon et al. 2011) Cultural discrimination: language, dress or cultural practices
	Integration of People from Disadvantaged Areas
Drivers	At the level of individuals: Mentoring: promotes the transmission of know-how (e.g. training low-skilled young people) (Montargot 2013; Sabouné 2016) or soft skills, with some young people having little experience. Some young school dropouts and those who have experienced difficulties in finding employment may also seek psychological support to help their integration and to overcome a lack of self-confidence Friendly welcome and organization of federative events: this concerns some low-skilled youth (Dufour and Lacaze 2010; Montargot 2013; Sabouné 2016) Recognition of identity: social (young people), ethnic (those of non-European immigrant backgrounds), religious (Muslim faith), a posture of equality (some low-skilled youth) (Montargot 2013; Sabouné 2016) Work–life balance: financial, logistical (housing and transportation) and psychological support; some low-skilled youth face financial constraints, housing or transportation issues and family-related challenges that impact their professional well-being (Sabouné 2012, 2016) Meaning: having a stable job, as many young people have difficulty finding employment; acquiring a job that matches their skills, as some young graduates have to work in a job that is often far below their qualifications; having a job characterized by the presence of rewarding, diverse tasks or even with connections, as many low-skilled young people work in jobs marked by the presence of devaluing tasks (Dufour and Lacaze 2010; Sabouné 2016)
Drivers	Remuneration: remuneration in line with the efforts invested by many low-skilled youth (Dufour and Lacaze 2010; Montargot 2013; Sabouné 2016) or with the educational capital held (many young people are indeed graduates) Professional development: equality in terms of professional development, as some people are discriminated against in this respect because of their origin
Obstacles	At the individual level: cultural demands that do not line up with the organizational culture, social assistance from a public institution or more or less legal remuneration. The majority of these people are young people with few qualifications On the organizational side: the economic imperatives faced by some managers; the professional or cultural expectations of some young people that are not met

Table 1.1. *Initial approach to the drivers of and obstacles to recruitment and integration of people from disadvantaged areas in the literature*

1.2.1. Recruitment

Several exogenous factors have led companies to recruit from this type of population, including the specific characteristics of the sector of activity, which requires attracting young people with low qualifications due to retirement or the use of immigrant populations due to unattractive working conditions. A second factor relates to the influence exerted by the business sector. Due to its location in an area with a significant immigrant population, company B is accustomed to recruiting employees from this population. At the same time, the head of this company hopes that it will enjoy the recognition of the local community and that its employees will be able to carry out their activities in this area without fear of reprisals from certain young people living there. Like the manager of company A, the manager of company B adopted this type of recruitment to limit the distance between home and work for his employees, and, at the same time, increase their productivity at work. A final factor relates to the role played by public incentives. By recruiting in these areas, these companies receive financial aid from the State. For example, when it was eligible to obtain a public contract, company B was obligated to hire a certain number of young people who were far from employment. It also faced administrative constraints concerning the recruitment of foreign workers: "Who can we recruit today, if not the young people around us? We hear about waves of migration, but getting the correct identity papers to get the right to work is not as easy as it used to be" (manager from company B). Like company A, company B signed the company and territory charter to promote local employment. In participating in employment forums organized in honor of these young people, or by subscribing to the "Young People Professional Guarantee" scheme, company A also committed itself to acting in this direction.

The managers of these companies also played a very important role in the choice of this source of recruitment. They were convinced of the qualities of these young people, even less young people, from these urban areas. The manager of company A saw young people as serious, loyal, captivating, lively and as having a singular will to get by, while the manager of company B said that it is "really important that its managers [...] come from these priority neighborhoods", "[...] a Maghrebi from the Maghreb [...] the relationship they will have together will be a cultural one that will allow them to talk, [...] to integrate into the company much more easily". As they themselves come from these urban areas and are connected to them, these managers wanted to promote local employment: "Since I'm from the priority neighborhoods,

95% of my employees are also from the priority neighborhoods." For the manager of company A: "it's difficult for a young person from the area to create his or her own structure [...], because [...] the public service has created institutional racism: [...] these young people, for the boys, will be offered anything in the field of security; and for the women, they are always offered cleaning". Consequently, the manager of company A considered it necessary to create an association to promote the effective recruitment of these young people. This was confirmed by one of the young people working there: "In this company, they have a training center [...] which favors young people from the suburbs [...]; they train you and then they hire you" (research manager, 31 years old).

The managers at the head of the two companies did not hesitate to influence the recruitment policy of other managers who were not accustomed to recruiting people from these territories. Finally, while they worked to recruit these young people by using legal or ad hoc measures (such as social clauses or the "Young People Professional Guarantee"), they refused to participate in certain measures, such as employment forums, considering that it was a way for companies to promote only their brand image. As some of them confided to us, they were not able to participate in any of these programs. As some employees told us, while the manager in charge alone knows this recruitment policy within company B, other organizational actors were responsible for relaying it correctly within company A. One of them told us that he was doing this both because of the organizational culture instilled by his company and because of his personal experience: "Our goal is to get young people out of Seine-Saint-Denis [...] because we realize that there is discrimination and that there is a way for young people to get out of it. [...] Even for me, though I'm blond and blue-eyed, when I applied to [a school that trains beauticians]; ... when they saw my CV with Saint-Ouen on it, ... people were reticent" (executive assistant, 28 years old).

1.2.2. *Integration*

Two factors in company B's external environment clearly influenced its integration policy aimed at young unemployed people. The first was the lack of an available workforce and the importance of doing everything possible to keep young people in work: "Young people in integration are like teenagers who go off the rails; you have to [...] always talk, not get discouraged [...].

The company has no choice but to renew and enrich itself," and it has the desire "[...] to work [...] in sensitive areas" (the manager). The historical integration of company B within this territory plays an important role in the promotion of employees who come from this area, as an employee working for an association in partnership with the company told us.

Where the managers at the head of the companies studied play an important role in the integration of this type of population, they advocate within their respective companies for mutual support and respect for the young recruits. They also insist on the attention that all their employees should give to the support of these young, poorly qualified and inexperienced employees, considering that "what the State or the school has not done, or has done badly, the company must do" and that "in some neighborhoods, the parents have given up". Not only do the managers at the head of the companies make the most experienced employees aware of the need to support them, but they also force them to act in this direction. Several employees told us that they had been supported by a mentor or their colleagues when they joined the company. This support took three forms. First, this support took a cognitive form, which involved passing on knowledge to the young employees (e.g. ICT skills), teaching them interpersonal skills and the correct etiquette. In this case, the majority of young people with little experience were involved. For example, one interviewee told us that he was on first-name terms with his manager and used atypical language with him. A young woman, whose professional prospects could be improved by acquiring more qualifications and a higher level of education, told us that this type of support was necessary to improve her written expression and grammar. As such, the manager of company A did not hesitate to offer social advice to certain young people, such as the fact that they should be educated. The second type of support offered to unemployed young people was in the form of psychological support that relied on the use of a very particular language and empathy. Young people who have experienced difficulties in finding employment may necessarily benefit from this type of support in order to help them regain their self-confidence. Finally, we can identify an emotional form of support, which took the shape of an inclusive organizational climate and inclusive events designed to help these young people integrate better into the company.

Despite such professional support, some young employees persistently adopted inappropriate professional behaviors shortly after joining the company or even several years later. For various reasons, some organizational actors were able to demonstrate tolerance: "Sometimes I arrive late, but he [the company director] isn't going to yell at me [...]; he knows that sooner or later, if he needs me, I will stay for a meeting or whatever" (project assistant). This could also be for ethical reasons, such as prioritizing the organizational culture: "We're kind of like a family business, we want to support young people from disadvantaged neighborhoods" (executive assistant); or identification with the issues that these young people faced: "I would like to work, so that people don't say 'these Arabs, these black people don't work'" (team leader, 38 years old, company B). Finally, this could be because of perceived support when they arrived in the company: "He [an employee of the company] is the one who made me have entrepreneurial spirit. In fact, I trained him [and] helped him express himself better since he had difficulty expressing himself" (Telecom research officer).

On the other hand, some managers are not able to provide long-term support to certain low-skilled young people for two main reasons. The first is economic constraints; for example, company B lacked the financial resources to ensure long-term employment of certain young people recruited through the social integration program. The second reason is lack of experience or interpersonal skills, which sometimes results in a failure to respect schedules, repeated absences and violent behavior towards other employees: "They fought with us" (site manager, 47 years old); or displayed dangerous behavior in the workplace: "It's the young people who are smokers and drinkers that upset the working environment" (manager, company A).

Based on these observations, we observed that a mentor can help the integration of employees from these territories only up to a certain extent. In short, if the fact of promoting cultural proximity between the former and the latter can also be a catalyst for this type of integration, as one employee confided to us: "It is an example of the success of a guy [the company manager] from the suburbs [...]; I'm not going to denigrate it" (researcher); diversity at work can also be as one of the managers interviewed described: "It is part of our policy to mix mentalities [...]; if you put [...] three young girls who have lived in a housing estate [...], the language will not be sustained" (company A).

However, a cultural distance between a young person from these territories and their manager (company B) or the culture of a company

(company A) can be an obstacle to their integration in the company. Indeed, some people have been harassed or even shunned because of their social origin: "We are stigmatized here; so a site manager, who comes from the Oise, says to himself: 'ugh… a youth from a neighborhood', the label; the site managers are turning heads" (works manager, 29 years old); or ethnicity: "There was a boss, a very racist Frenchman, who spoke to me very badly [...]; besides, [...] I would have fought with him if there was no one there; it was people who separated us [and my work supervisor] who took me out of that team" (assistant supervisor, 23 years old, company B). For others, who are Muslim, the manager of company A was reluctant to accommodate their needs regarding Friday prayer. In these companies, some young people were also ostracized by certain employees because of their lack of professional experience. At the same time, it seems that these managers or other employees remain open to ethnic diversity and, to a certain extent, religion: "At company B, [...] there has never been any discrimination and my mentor wears a veil" (accounting assistant, age 19). In our two companies, some managers also seemed to accept the adoption of a posture of equality towards young people.

Some employees from these areas also faced difficulties outside of work. These could be material (e.g. financial, housing, and transportation difficulties, etc.). To help them overcome these difficulties, the managers sometimes assisted them with their own means: "He lends money to struggling workers" (work supervisor, 58 years old, company B); "He helps the workers [...]." "He helps workers [...] in difficulty, especially with housing" (team leader, 38 years old); "I saw young people who were a bit outside the system [...]; they were given the chance to work [and] paid for driver's licenses" (chief mechanic, 59 years old).

These difficulties could also be intangible. The managers of companies A and B were flexible about regularizing the administrative situation of people with an immigrant background: "A Malian worked with us for two years; afterwards, they discovered that the card was a fake: they fired him not even two weeks later, he got the card, and they made another appointment for him" (team leader, 38 years old, company B); and overcoming the legal problems of unemployed young people: "There may be young people [...], when they have entered working life, [...] [whose] friends are hanging around doing stupid things [...]; then it's the clink; [...] I write to the judge,

[…] because I have invested in him; and often the response to this investment is good" (company B). These managers were also able to grant leave abroad to immigrant workers in case of family problems: "If a worker needs [the company manager], he goes to see him. For example, his mother died in Mali, so a young man asked for three months; he went on vacation for three months" (site manager, 47 years old). Some young people with few qualifications, working in company A, told us that they had sought psychological support from their manager in order to overcome uneasiness at work resulting from family problems. The director of company A could support the entrepreneurship of some young people who had left their company: "Some young people will tell me that they are going to create their own company; […] I will support them as best I can."

With regard to their professional situation within the companies studied, the young employees that we interviewed all told us that they were in a stable professional situation due to the employment policy of the managers interviewed, which sought to promote professional stability among their employees. Others had a job that matched their skills and the responsibilities associated with it (these were young people with degrees) or a job with positive characteristics: meaningful, diversified and contactable tasks (some young people with few qualifications). On the other hand, many low-skilled young people have left company B to do "easier work" (team leader). Regarding the remuneration policy in the companies studied, the interviewees did not consider it to be discriminatory. However, while the employees interviewed generally said that they felt that they were paid fairly, others, especially young people who were mostly unskilled, left the company because they deemed the remuneration insufficient, and left in favor of higher pay from another company. Some low-skilled young people have left company B to receive social assistance: "Some come to fulfil their quota of hours vis-à-vis the Assedic […]; [then] they don't come at all" (team leader, 46 years old). Others leave as they prefer remuneration of an illicit nature: "The salary […] does not please [them] [laughs] compared to what they earn quickly" (team leader, 38 years old).

Finally, as far as their professional development is concerned, some employees from these urban areas have confided that their experiences have met their expectations. One of the factors that seems to have favored their career development within these two companies is the commitment of the manager: "Management goes for it. [There are quite a few guys, who are from the area, [who] [...] started out as laborers; they ended up as site managers" (site manager, 58 years old); another is the organizational culture: "I think that we evolve on merit" (team leader, 37 years old). On the other hand, in company B, some employees confided that they had been discriminated against in terms of promotion because of their geographical origin: "I came in as a bricklayer; when there is no site manager, I manage; but to get this grade, no: [...] I have a site manager [decrease in voice] [who] hates Arabs and blacks" (bricklayer, 50 years old, company B).

In the end, we observed that a certain number of managerial practices affecting the professional, socio-cultural and social identity of employees recruited helped improved their professional integration according to their social profile. While some organizational actors have been in favor of this type of integration for economic and cultural reasons, it has also encountered several obstacles.

1.3. Contextualizing the inclusion of people from disadvantaged territories

Our empirical results are consistent with other research already being done in this area and can also be extended to support inclusion initiatives on a territory.

1.3.1. *Supporting urban recruitment through SMEs*

Several of our findings regarding the recruitment of the target population are supported by research in this area (Angotti et al. 2007; Labulle 2013; Mathivet and Raoul-Chassaing 2016; Jardat and Labulle 2018). Among these results, some touch upon exogenous factors close to those influencing diversity policy (Bruna et al. 2017): the situation of the sector of activity, the integration to a territory, the search for geographical proximity to employees, the obtaining of a public contract and the institutional injunctions of the moment (Paradas 2008; Bonneveux et al. 2011; Delchet-Cochet and Vo 2012; Bon et al. 2015).

However, our results allow us to identify new drivers and obstacles regarding recruitment. Some of these do not seem to be specific to SMEs:

the administrative constraints involved in recruiting a foreign workforce, although large companies are better equipped to overcome these constraints.

Others, on the other hand, seem to be linked to two of the specific characteristics of the SME. The first is tied to the control that the managers interviewed have over recruitment, since they are in a position that allows them to prioritize people from these urban areas when hiring. In addition to the reasons mentioned above, we have seen that other reasons led these managers to act in this way relating to their social origin, personal experience, social commitment and other more instrumental reasons, which are tied to the other qualities of these populations. Our research also shows that such directors did not hesitate to influence the recruitment of managers who are not used to opening up to this type of population (Bruna et al. 2017). For example, one of the directors implemented an innovative structure to promote inclusion. These findings confirm that an SME is able to adopt innovative autonomous social commitment (Berger-Douce 2008, 2009).

The second characteristic of SMEs relates to the commitment shared by the managers for recruitment of this kind. We can thus assume that, in addition to the social profile of the managers in charge of relaying this recruitment, the director had, due to the number of managers invested in this approach, an easier time disseminating their managerial convictions to them (Mahé de Boislandelle 1998; Igalens et al. 2011). In large companies, managers' resistance to this type of recruitment can be strong (Labulle 2013) and so having managers from these urban areas becomes an asset for companies wishing to recruit from this population. Our study shows that, by recruiting managers from these urban areas, a company will be able to more easily overcome any resistance to the recruitment of people from these urban areas.

1.3.2. *Difficulties of employee inclusion*

Our results show that some employees, once recruited, were confronted with integration difficulties, leading the companies studied to adopt specific practices. While some of these practices have already been addressed in other works, for example, the offering of professional and emotional support or identity recognition (Labulle 2013; Montargot and Saboune 2014; Sabouné 2016; Jardat and Labulle 2018), our study sheds light on others, including fostering cultural homogeneity or diversity in the work environment; providing social support in the event of administrative, family or legal problems; and fostering the success of an entrepreneurial project. Similarly, while certain studies have made it possible to account for certain factors leading organizational actors to act in favor of this kind of integration, in particular the influence of the director or their identification with these young people (Labulle 2013; Jardat and Labulle 2018), our results have highlighted others. These are, once again, very similar factors to those that influence diversity policies (i.e. the sector of activity, the area of activity, the organizational culture and the perceived support upon arrival in a company). As far as the career development of people from these urban areas is concerned, one of their expectations that favors their integration, and our results confirm this (Labulle 2013), highlights the importance of the culture of these companies and the attitude of their managers.

Based on these different observations, we can once again see the influence that SME directors can have on inclusion. However, this is not the case in some companies, where, for example, the extra-professional difficulties that some people from these urban areas may face do not elicit a response from their managers (Labulle 2013). Our study also allows us to better understand the profiles of employees who are attached to a type of managerial practice. Indeed, the cognitive support provided by an organizational actor when teaching a skill or knowledge specific to the use of an ICT does not only concern young people and low-skilled young people, but also older people and more skilled young people, just as financial or housing support is not only expected by low-skilled young people, but also by people in low-skilled jobs. Finally, the organization of federative events is not only an aspiration of low-skilled young people but is also shared by young people with higher qualifications.

Finally, we can identify three obstacles specific to this type of social commitment. The first concerns the economic constraints that a company faces in recruiting young people in the process of professional integration, which confirms that an SME tends to prioritize the search for competitive advantages over the fulfillment of a social mission (Paradas 2008; Bonneveux et al. 2011; Delchet-Cochet and Vo 2012; Bon et al. 2015). The second concerns the internal resistance of some managers (Labulle 2013). In spite of the commitment of the managers interviewed on this subject, this confirms that, in adopting a policy of diversity, some SME managers may still face resistance from their own managers (Naschberger and Guerfel-Henda 2013). The third concerns the professional or cultural behavior of young people, their professional expectations and those of an extra-professional nature that cannot be met. This confirms that a company adopting such a policy cannot blindly ignore certain professional and social differences (Chanlat et al. 2013).

1.4. Conclusion

In light of these various observations, it appears that it is in a company's best interest to adopt practices dedicated to target populations as part of a social commitment to inclusion within a territory. While our research has confirmed what is already known about certain drivers of and obstacles to the inclusion of people from disadvantaged urban areas, it has also highlighted other drivers that are specific to this type of inclusion (such as the constraints of recruiting a certain type of workforce, certain characteristics of SMEs, etc.) and other integration practices and drivers of inclusion.

1.5. References

Angotti, M., David-Alberola, E., Loones, A. (2007). *Entreprises ordinaires, entreprises solidaires ? L'implication des entreprises dans l'insertion des publics éloignés de l'emploi.* CRÉDOC, Paris.

Barth, I. (2018). *Manager la diversité : de la lutte contre les discriminations au leadership inclusif.* Dunod, Paris.

Barth, I. and Falcoz, C. (2010). *Nouvelles perspectives en management de la diversité.* EMS, Caen.

Bender, A.F. and Pigeyre, F. (2010). Mieux conceptualiser la diversité : un enjeu de gestion. In *Mieux conceptualiser la diversité : un enjeu de gestion*, Barth, I. and Falcoz, C. (eds). EMS, Caen.

Berger-Douce, S. (2008). L'engagement sociétal d'une PME : une démarche au service de l'intégration professionnelle de publics en difficulté ? *Revue internationale de psychosociologie et de gestion des comportements organisationnels*, 14(32), 207–223.

Berger-Douce, S. (2009). La diversité en PME : une philosophie managériale au service de la performance ? *Management et Avenir*, 29, 258–274.

Bon, V., Pensel, J.L., Morlet, D. (2015). Les PME engagées en RSE : des clés de compréhension à partir d'une approche qualitative. *Recherches en sciences de gestion*, 109, 75–100.

Bonneveux, E., Calme, I., Soparnot, R. (2011). La diffusion d'une démarche RSE innovante au sein d'un réseau de PME : le cas du Centre des Jeunes Dirigeants. *Gestion 2000*, 28(2), 69–90.

Bruna, M.G., Frimousse, S., Giraud, L. (2017). Comment apprécier l'impact transformationnel d'une politique de diversité en entreprise ? *Contribution liminaire à un agenda de recherche, Management et avenir*, 96, 39–71.

Chanlat, J.F. and Özbilgin, M. (eds) (2018). *Management et diversité : comparaisons internationales*. Hermann, Paris.

Chanlat, J.F. and Özbilgin, M. (eds) (2019). *Management et diversité : approches thématiques et défis sociopolitiques*. Hermann, Paris.

Chanlat, J.F., Dameron, S., Dupuis, J.P., De Freitas, E.M., Özbilgin, M. (2013). Management et diversité : lignes de tension et perspectives. *Management International*, 17, 5–13.

Conseil économique et social (2008). L'emploi des jeunes des quartiers populaires. Notice, Conseil économique et social, 25.

Cusin, J. and Charreire-Petit, S. (2015). Vers l'identification des leviers, des risques et des arbitrages dans le déploiement d'une pratique RSE tournée vers les publics éloignés de l'emploi. *Revue de l'organisation responsable*, 10, 58–74.

Darriau, V., Henry, M., Oswalt, N. (2014). Politique de la ville en France métropolitaine : une nouvelle géographie recentrée sur 1300 quartiers prioritaires. *INSEE*, 151–153.

Delchet-Cochet, K. and Vo, L.C. (2012). Impact of CSR tools on SMEs: The case of global performance in France. *International Business Research*, 5(7), 50–55.

Dhaoudi, I. (2008). La conception politique de la responsabilité sociale de l'entreprise : vers un nouveau rôle de l'entreprise dans une société globalisée. *Revue de l'organisation responsable*, 3, 76–32.

Dufour, L. (2008). Les déterminants de l'intégration des jeunes à faible capital scolaire. PhD Thesis, Aix-Marseille University, Marseille.

Dufour, L. and Lacaze, D. (2010). L'intégration dans l'entreprise des jeunes à faible capital scolaire : un processus d'ajustement mutuel. *Revue de gestion des ressources humaines*, 75, 16–29.

Duport, M., Frimousse, S., Peretti, J.M. (2020). L'évolution du management de la diversité dans les entreprises (2007–2019). In *Approches critiques des organisations*, Pijoan, N. and Plane, J.M. (eds). EMS, Paris.

European Commission (2003). Décision de la Commission. Report, European Commission.

Gobillon, L., Magnac, T., Selod, H. (2011). La ségrégation résidentielle : un facteur de chômage ? *Regards croisés sur l'économie*, 9, 272–281.

Igalens, J., Louitri, A., Sahraoui, D. (2011). GRH et encadrement au féminin : cas d'une PME marocaine. *Management et Avenir*, 43, 82–102.

Jardat, R. and Labulle, F. (2018). Local inefficiencies in French public–private diversity and inclusion policies: Envisioning a locality-based intersectional analysis. *Society and Business Review*, 13(1), 39–60.

Labulle, F. (2013). GRH, diversité, et territoire : les pratiques de trois entreprises implantées à Aulnay-sous-Bois. PhD Thesis, Paris-East Créteil University, Paris.

Laïchour, L. (2020). Les facteurs d'inclusion et d'exclusion des personnes issues de territoires en difficulté : le cas de trois PME localisées en Seine-Saint-Denis. PhD Thesis, Paris Dauphine University, Paris.

Mahé de Boislandelle, H. (1998). GRH en PME. Universalité et contingences : essai de théorisation. *Revue internationale P.M.E.*, 11(2/3), 11–30.

Mathivet, C. and Raoul-Chassaing, I. (2016). Recruter, recruté(e)s, recrutez, … dans les quartiers ? Favoriser le recrutement dans les quartiers prioritaires de la politique de la Ville, regards croisés d'entreprises. Report, Lab'Ho, Observatoire des Hommes et des organisations.

Montargot, N. (2013). L'intégration des jeunes à faible capital scolaire : le cas de l'Hôtellerie-Restauration. PhD Thesis, Cergy-Pontoise University, Cergy.

Montargot, N. and Saboune, K. (2014). Gérer la diversité dans les organisations par la connaissance des attentes individuelles : le cas des jeunes à faible capital scolaire initial. *Management et Avenir*, 74, 15–32.

Naschberger, C. and Guerfel-Henda, S. (2013). La mise en œuvre d'une démarche diversité en PME – Quelques enseignements d'un centre d'appel spécialisé. *Management International*, 17, 98–112.

Paradas, A. (2008). La position des petites entreprises face à la responsabilité sociale. *Revue de l'organisation responsable*, 3(1), 39–52.

Peretti, J.M. (1994). *Ressources Humaines*. Vuibert, Paris.

Sabouné, K. (2012). Réflexions sur la réussite de l'insertion professionnelle : contribution à l'étude des attentes des jeunes sans qualification. Le cas de formations de la région Poitou-Charentes. PhD Thesis, University of Poitiers, Poitiers.

Sabouné, K. (2016). Contribution à l'audit du contrat psychologique chez les jeunes sans qualification en formation. *Question(s) de management*, 13, 11–22.

Tatli, A. and Özbilgin, M.F. (2009). Understanding diversity managers' role in organizational change: Towards a conceptual framework. *Canadian Journal of Administrative Sciences*, 26, 244–258.

2

"Territories with Zero Long-Term Unemployment" through the Lens of Neo-Institutional Theory

In this chapter, we examine the process deployed by an organization for the building, adoption and diffusion of an inclusive practice on a territory through the lens of neo-institutional theory. Adopting a holistic approach, we conduct our analysis at two levels (Lawrence et al. 2011): the institutional level of exogenous macro-influences and the level of endogenous micro-actions developed by the various actors who are the bearers of the approach.

First, we define the concept of inclusion and clarify its evolution in order to present the social enterprise and identify the actors involved in the process of promoting inclusion. Then, drawing on concepts from neo-institutional theory, we examine how an emerging inclusive practice gains its legitimacy, which ensures its adoption and implementation at the territorial to the national levels. Finally, we present the case of a specific inclusion scheme in France known as *"Territoires zéro chômeur de longue durée"* (TZCLDs) or territories with zero long-term unemployment, which aimed at eradicating long-term unemployment. The first experiment was carried out in 10 territories and was then extended to a larger scale.

Chapter written by Amina SAYDI and Martine BRASSEUR.

2.1. Inclusive practice

An inclusive practice within a territory is a practice that aims to make inclusion a reality at the local level. As a concept, inclusion is subject to much debate, and like any recently developed concept, its meaning and value are only as strong as the scope and power it is given (Gardou 2012).

2.1.1. *Inclusion*

"Inclusion" is a concept that denotes the presence of positive social goodwill with the aim of solving social and economic problems. Its fundamental issue concerns the challenge of ensuring equality of opportunity, or, as it is more widely known, the idea of "everything for each person" (Bauer 2015). At the European level, the term "inclusion" was first used to refer to the fight against poverty and then expanded to include specific actions aimed at supporting particular groups. Social inclusion is defined as "a process that ensures that people at risk of poverty and exclusion get the opportunities and resources they need so as to be able to participate fully in economic, social, and cultural life" (Bouquet 2015, p. 18).

In order to establish this objective of operationalization, the European Union (EU) adopted a political project at the European Council meeting in Lisbon in 2000 entitled "Building an Inclusive Europe"[1] and continued with its Europe 2020 strategy for "smart, sustainable and inclusive growth"[2]. The exercise of inclusion in such projects allows it to adhere to structural programs and to benefit from peer review at the national levels of Member States, notably through the Open Method of Coordination (OMC), an instrument of the Lisbon 2000 strategy. The OMC is implemented for areas that fall within the competence of the EU countries, such as employment, social protection, social inclusion, education, youth and vocational training[3].

The concept of inclusion is gradually replacing the concepts of integration and insertion (Ebersold 2009). However, Gardou (2012) makes a

---

1 See: https://www.europarl.europa.eu/summits/lis1_fr.htm (accessed: September 21, 2021).
2 See: https://www.enseignementsup-recherche.gouv.fr/cid71587/la-strategie-europe-2020-pour-une-growth-smart-sustainable-and-inclusive.html (accessed September 21, 2021).
3 See: https://eur-lex.europa.eu/summary/glossary/open_method_coordination.html?locale=fr (accessed: September 21, 2021).

distinction between the concepts of integration and inclusion, which are different in terms of the normalization effort required of actors:

> The objective of integration is to bring into a whole, to incorporate. It is a matter of assembling the different constituent parts of a system, ensuring their compatibility and the proper functioning of the whole. In contrast, a social organization is inclusive when it modulates its functioning, making itself flexible to offer, within the common whole, a "home for all", Without neutralizing singular needs, desires or destinies and resorbing them in the whole (Gardou 2012, pp. 36–37).

This distinction is consistent with the definition that places inclusion at high levels of belonging and uniqueness, where "the individual is treated as an insider and is also authorized and encouraged to maintain their uniqueness within the working group" (Shore et al. 2010, p. 1266).

As such, inclusion is an indifference to difference and an acceptance of everyone. The resurgence of the concept of inclusion in the political discourse testifies to a change of perspective at both the social and economic levels and an urgency of action at the local level to include all social strata for a more equitable society through the achievement of a common base of identical rights for all. The manifestation of this concept in political discourse also speaks to the need for institutional ownership due to the lack of primary solidarities (Gardien 2015).

2.1.2. *The social enterprise*

The adoption of the "social and solidarity economy" (SSE) law in July 2014 marked the institutionalization of inclusive practice[4]. The SSE is a third sector located between the public economy and the private economy (Glémain 2019). Authors such as the American political scientist James Burnham, in his 1941 book *The Managerial Revolution*, had already denied the capitalist–socialist dilemma and believed in the advent of a third regime. The questioning of capitalism and its excesses is also one of the topics

---

4 See: https://www.legifrance.gouv.fr/affichTexte.do?cidTexte=JORFTEXT000029313296&categorieLien=id (accessed: October 21, 2021).

addressed by *Critical Management Studies*, in which "the focus is more on the concepts of power, control, inequality and domination than on those of efficiency and competitiveness" (Huault 2008, p. 318).

This strand, which puts current management challenges into perspective, aims to denounce social injustice. Thanks to the law of July 2014, the social enterprise was able to structure itself. Social enterprises are "these enterprises of people, which are under associative, cooperative, mutualist or foundation status" (Glémain 2019, p. 57). Through social enterprise, the practice of inclusion can be established. "Social enterprises innovate socially, promote inclusion and reinforce trust" (Eynaud and Mourey 2015, p. 86). These enterprises also display agency competencies and develop relationships with state and local governments, on the one hand, and with the SSE sector, on the other hand.

This legal recognition reflects a certain willingness to consider social enterprises involved in solidarity as full partners in social inclusion. The SSE is complementarity to the state logic of public utility and that of the market and the profit of the private sector. A social enterprise is, like any enterprise of the market economy, organized around the *affectio societatis*, which designates the common will between several moral or legal persons to form an association[5]. *Affectio societatis* reflects shared values and the deliberate pursuit of a common interest (Glémain 2019), which expresses a willingness to invest and share through collective action by several actors. In addition to this common attribute with market enterprises, the social enterprise is distinguished by a mode of governance that is part of a participatory dynamic, hence the need for articulation between the social enterprise and the public power and the importance of the social project carried by the groups that constitute it (Eynaud and Mourey 2015). The participatory dimension of the social enterprise gives considerable importance to the role of the actors who constitute it.

2.2. The perspective of neo-institutional theory

Neo-institutional theory concerns the social conformity and the observation of the isomorphism phenomena of fairly mature organizational domains (Greenwood et al. 2002; Maguire et al. 2004). It emphasizes the

---

5 See: https://www.dictionnaire-juridique.com/definition/affectio-societatis.php (accessed: October 21, 2020).

constraints imposed by institutions and the rules that guide behavior and claims that "[i]nstitutions are not only constraints on human agency; they are first and foremost products of human activity" (DiMaggio and Powell 1991, p. 28).

2.2.1. *The institution as a product of actors*

Early work within the neo-institutional framework abandoned the role of human action in the formation of institutions in favor of a macrosociological approach (Taupin 2017). As DiMaggio and Powell (1991, p. 16) point out, "[w]e argue that the macro side of neo-institutionalism is central. Yet any macrosociology draws on microsociology, however tacitly."

In sociology, a "role" is defined as the mediating link between the individual and the social system (Luhmann 1996). Thus, "[i]nstitutional strategies represent attempts by actors to change the nature of competition in their industry, either through membership rules or its standards of practice" (Lawrence 1999, p. 169). The institutional entrepreneurship concept has enabled reintroducing the role of actors into neo-institutional analysis (DiMaggio 1988). This concept explains the contribution of actors in changing institutions despite pressures of stagnation (Battilana et al. 2009). According to Fligstein (1997), institutional entrepreneurship has placed the actor at the heart of institutional theory because it is narrow in scope, focusing not on actors but on how the meanings of their actions are valued in the organizational field. For Hwang and Powell (2005), this concept considers the individual as the primary unit for creating new activities and highlights the particular capacity of certain actors to create new institutions. "New institutions arise when organized actors with sufficient resources see in them an opportunity to realize interests that they value highly" (DiMaggio 1988, p. 14).

The action of actors has since gradually gained importance in institutional research. Institutional work, a new concept which represents a broader category of actions that actors may perform, can be defined as "[t]he purposive action of individuals and organizations aimed at creating, maintaining, and disrupting institutions" (Lawrence and Suddaby 2006, p. 215). In addition to characterizing institution building as institutional entrepreneurship, institutional work is also about sustaining and disrupting its existence, and even about its demise. In their book, Lawrence et al. (2009) make a crucial distinction for the study of institutional work between the creation, maintenance and disruption of institutions. The first two terms describe a set of activities, while the latter refers to a set of activity outcomes. Consequently, the issues raised are different. According to the authors, this distinction points to what they call "unintended consequences" that may emerge during the creation of intended institutional effects.

The level of analysis of the neo-institutional theoretical framework is important to note: "It represents an intermediate level between the organization and society and plays a role in the processes by which socially structured expectations and practices disseminate and reproduce" (Greenwood et al. 2002, p. 58). The neo-institutional approach focuses its analysis more on interorganizational systems than the internal dynamics of an organization (Selznick 1949): "This intermediate level of analysis focuses on the entirety of the relevant actors structuring a system, which operates according to its own logic, beyond the sole economic-competitive domain" (Huault 2017, p. 170).

The two concepts of institutional entrepreneurship and institutional work show the breadth of actors' actions: "These practices go well beyond those of institutional entrepreneurs – the creation of new institutions requires institutional work by a wide range of actors, both those with the resources and skills to act entrepreneurs and those whose role supports or facilitates the entrepreneur's efforts" (Lawrence and Suddaby 2006, p. 217).

2.2.2. Actors initiating change

Whether it is the individual action of a few isolated figures, as in institutional entrepreneurship, or the more collective actions of institutional work, neo-institutional theory demonstrates that some actors are more successful than others in producing social outcomes (Fligstein 1997). According to this approach, the actors who accomplish change are distinguished from others in terms of their resources. Coleman (1988) describes them as actors with a high level of social capital. The author distinguishes between three forms of resources: physical capital, which is created by changing materials to form tools for production; human capital, which is embodied in the skills, abilities and knowledge of the actors; and social capital, which is the result of changes in the relationships between people that facilitate action. Social capital is as productive as the other two forms of capital but is less tangible and non-fungible – it is not found in the tools of production or in the actors themselves and is specific to certain activities. According to Fligstein (1997, p. 107), resourceless actors are the ones who are most often constrained by institutions, but in some circumstances, they may unintentionally use existing rules to create new institutions. In addition to considering resources and rules as constitutive elements of social life, the capacity of actors to use them is added in neo-institutional theories. This social competence has the advantage of being considered within a collective and can help to "engage others in collective action [...] which proves essential to the construction and reproduction of local social orders" (Fligstein 1997, pp. 105–106).

The collective dimension is essential for successful institutional arrangements that give rise to social orders, which are defined as "situations in which organized groups of actors come together and define their actions in relation to each other" (Fligstein 1997, p. 108). These local social orders be referred to by several different terms: "fields" (Bourdieu 1997), "organizational fields" (DiMaggio and Powell 1983), and "sectors" (Meyer and Scott 1983).

Human actions, or agency, are micro-processes that drive the macro-influences that are institutions. Actors thus play an essential role in institutional work:

> Human agency can be seen as a temporally embedded process of social engagement informed by the past (in its habitual aspect), as well as one oriented toward the future (as a capacity to imagine alternative possibilities) and toward the present (as a capacity to contextualize past habits and future projects within the contingencies of the moment) (Emirbayer and Mische 1998, p. 963).

This definition highlights the notion of temporality of action that is essential in social life, especially during critical moments such as "test" moments that can characterize the emergence of an institution.

In conventionalist theory, "[a] test is a moment of questioning of value frameworks or their forms of instantiation in which actors seek to confirm or determine the principles, or the 'orders of worth', that ought to apply in a given situation" (Dansou and Langley 2012, p. 511). The questioning of the institutional arrangements that approve the test allows for an evaluation of actions at the micro level and principles at the macro level. This is an extraordinary opportunity for the actors to establish the modalities of their common actions in a different way: "In these moments, actors seek to confirm or choose to confront the way in which institutional rules, norms or accepted beliefs are instantiated in particular situations. [...] when institutional solidity and plasticity are assessed, and their confirmation or alteration is played out" (Dansou and Langley 2012, p. 504). Testing offers the opportunity for isolation from the space of experimentation. This autonomy can allow for the development of practices that are not possible in a standard organization with predetermined and fixed modes of action. Experimentation thus allows us to free ourselves from institutions in the sense of the presence of authoritative rules or a constraining organization (Jepperson 1991). The test thus makes it possible to initiate change. It is a time when challenges may arise for the course of action (Dansou and Langley 2012). It symbolizes an opportunity for actors to change current practices and readjust their current strategies.

2.2.3. The contributions of neo-institutional theory to the question of the diffusion of inclusive practices

An institutional strategy is a set of "patterns of organizational action which are concerned with the formation and transformation of institutions, domains and the rules and standards that control those structures" (Lawrence 1999, p. 167). It allows us to describe the patterns of organizational action and reflects the process through which particular rules, practices or organizational forms become legitimized or desirable. An institutional strategy is an emergent strategy that includes two categories of precepts: rules of membership and norms of practice (Lawrence 1999). The goal is to transform new rules or typifications (Berger and Luckmann 1967) into institutionalized rules or reciprocal typifications. This strategy reflects the process of institutionalization, which "[...] occurs whenever there is a reciprocal typification of habitualized actions by types of actors. [...] What must be stressed is the reciprocity of institutional typifications and the typicality of not only the actions but also the actors in institutions" (Berger and Luckmann 1967, p. 72). It is a "[p]henomenological process by which certain social relationships and actions come to be taken for granted" (DiMaggio and Powell 1991, p. 9). It is the introduction of new rules within "dominant rationalized concepts", which are terms and knowledge embedded in a network associated with a particular organizational form or purpose (Lawrence 1999). This characterization of new rules allows new institutions to emerge and for new practices to be recognized and even adopted by institutions that are well integrated into the organizational field.

These new institutions are called "proto-institutions": "[t]hese new practices, technologies, and rules are institutions in the making: they have the potential to become full-fledged institutions if social processes develop that intrench them and they are diffused throughout an institutional field" (Lawrence et al. 2002, p. 283).

Proto-institutions are emerging institutions that are in the early stages of their institutionalization process, and in order to be legitimate, they must be replicated and diffused. The goal of the proto-institution is to progressively build trust in order to gain support within the organizational field where it interacts. It must be legitimate. Legitimacy refers to the idea of recognition and belonging to an organizational field. To acquire it, a new institution must overcome "the liability of newness", since "new organizations are thought to have a lower chance of survival because they must learn new roles without having role models, and they must establish ties with an environment that does not understand or acknowledge their existence" (Aldrich and Fiol 1994, p. 648). There are two dimensions of legitimacy: a cognitive dimension, which denotes knowledge of the new activity and what is needed to succeed (Aldrich and Fiol 1994), and a sociopolitical one, which represents the value placed on an activity by cultural norms and political authorities (Ranger-Moore et al. 1991). In summary, two questions can illustrate this typology of legitimacy: "where can I go?" and "what can I do?" (Lawrence 1999).

The motivation for a new practice is to improve performance, but it is its diffusion that gives it legitimacy. "As an innovation spreads, a threshold is reached beyond which adoption provides legitimacy rather than improving performance" (DiMaggio and Powell 1983, p. 148). Practices can thus be more or less institutionalized, depending on the extent of their diffusion. Diffusion occurs when "an innovation is communicated through certain channels over time between the members of a social system" (Rogers 1962, p. 14). Therefore, diffusion occurs in the direction of social relations and offers the opportunity for network analysis. It characterizes a spatial process, i.e. a transmission in terms of geographical distance among structurally equivalent actors (Strang and Meyer 1993).

This further detail allows us to distinguish between two levels of analysis: (1) the rule, the practice or the technology to be diffused; (2) the population for which this innovation is intended. This distinction is all the more important when the object of diffusion is theorized, as it allows for a better adaptation of the object to be adopted. This involves the "development and specification of abstract categories and the formulation of structured relationships such as chains of cause and effect" (Strang and Meyer 1993, p. 104). The role of theorizing is crucial for diffusion, as it enables a general model to be established, which makes the theory a mechanism or even a central channel for diffusion. According to these authors, theories of diffusion highlight the rationalities involved through certain benefits: identifying the characteristics of widespread practices, seeing the effectiveness or efficiency in relation to alternatives, developing coherence with previous attitudes or policies and making the new practice simpler. All of these benefits facilitate rational choice, make experimentation possible and provide the opportunity to learn from the experiences of others.

2.3. Case study: the territories with zero long-term unemployment experiment

In this section, we examine the construction of the experimental project represented by TZCLDs and the process of its institutionalization and its diffusion. How can the barriers of legitimacy be overcome in order to establish a new set of norms, paving the way for the growth of a new form of social entrepreneurship? Through the lens of neo-institutional theory, we also highlight the important role of actors in the system. Their mobilization within territories embodies the dynamics of the program's underlying mechanism.

2.3.1. *A collective approach for another way to achieve entrepreneurship*

TZCLDs are a French public policy program introduced following Law 2016-231, which was passed on February 29, 2016. It was an experiment in 10 territories that was conducted over a period of five years. Its aim was to make work a factor of social inclusion. Eradicating long-term unemployment (unemployment for more than a year) would make it possible to eliminate any possible cause of exclusion that may hinder access to the labor market for job seekers who have been unemployed for more than a year and to allow access to the labor market for populations usually excluded from it.

As part of the TZCLD experiment, each designated territory has seen the creation of one or two employment-oriented businesses (EOBs) with the ambition of achieving two distinct goals: the first is the "elimination of long-term unemployment" and the second is the "maintenance of the elimination of long-term unemployment", i.e. offering employment to the newly unemployed on a long-term basis. The fundamental principles driving the action of an EOB are: the exhaustiveness of recruitment in the territory tested, non-selective employment, the use of a common law permanent contract, availability according to the labor needs of the economy, net job creation and local experimentation (Valentin 2013).

EOBs are part of the SSE. Together, they represent a specific form of entrepreneurship that is part of a post-normative logic. EOBs are a new generation of enterprises; they are a form of proto-institutions that benefit from the financial support of the state but that in the long-term must reach autonomous financial equilibrium and be able to self-finance. An EOB falls into the category of associative enterprises, one of the four types of social enterprises that structure the SSE: the associative enterprise, the cooperative enterprise, the mutualist enterprise and the foundation.

EOBs were created as part of the TZCLD experiment by two associations that were both created in 2016: the ETCLD association (*"Expérimentation territoriale contre le chômage longue durée"*), which manages the ongoing experiment, and the TZCLD association (*"Territoires zéro chômeur de longue durée"*), which is responsible for obtaining the necessary funding (Valentin 2013). The EOB is the instrument of action for the experimentation in the territory: "It must recruit, without selection, all people who are permanently unemployed in the territory, and offer them a job on a voluntary basis in the fields of activity corresponding to the skills and desires of these people" (Hédon et al. 2019, p. 223). The choice of EOB activities is made at the level of the local committee with respect for a condition of non-competition with for-profit enterprises established in the intervention territory.

Another activity clause that must be observed by the EOB given its objective of eliminating long-term unemployment is that of not laying off its employees, except in extreme cases. Through these principles of non-selection, no-layoffs and non-competition with already established profit-making activities, etc., the EOB invents a business model that disrupts employment and reverses the logic of both the private and public sectors.

Denys Cordonnier, a member of the local committee in Colombey-les-Belles (54), notes that "[w]e don't take existing positions to fill them, we take existing people to create positions" (Hédon et al. 2019, p. 224). The economist Xavier Godinot (1995) speaks of an "inclusive" enterprise.

The financing of the TZCLD experimentation occurs within the framework of the right to experimentation of territorial authorities, which has been written into the constitution since 2003[6]. This was the case with the RSA experimentation before its adoption. Initially, it was financed by the state, but it will eventually be fed by the potential savings from the abolition of long-term unemployment in the experimental territory (Valentin 2018).

2.3.2. An experiment in search of diffusion

The TZCLD initiative is based on a dual model: it is both inclusive for the long-term unemployed for whom it is intended and participatory because it involves social partners from different backgrounds: ATD Fourth World, later joined by Secours Catholique, Emmaüs, the Fédération des acteurs de la solidarité and the Pacte Civique. This territory project is implemented by a steering committee in which all of the political and social actors of the territory are represented: parties, unions, associations, companies, chambers of commerce, municipalities, etc.

The EOBs created as part of the TZCLD experiment are legal entities in a test period. In this decisive and critical period, they must prove themselves in order to become full-fledged institutions. The test is a moment of ongoing questioning that offers the chance to experiment and find the right methods. The purpose of an EOB is more social than economic since its aim is to create employment opportunities rather than to promote economic competitiveness. Job creation is a pressing economic necessity. According to ATD Fourth World, long-term unemployment costs a staggering EUR 30 billion every year (Valentin 2013). Thanks to the principle of non-competition, the jobs created by an EOB are qualified as additional jobs commensurate with the needs of the territory until the list of volunteers is exhausted. A supplementary job does not generate unemployment elsewhere.

---

6 See: https://www.senat.fr/rap/l02-408/l02-4089.html (accessed: October 21, 2020).

Thus, the jobs generated by the EOBs are not a threat to private and/or public sector jobs[7].

The originality of the TZCLD experiment through the EOBs is that employment is conceived as a right for all long-term unemployed people. In fact, it simply applies a principle enshrined in the constitution: each person has the duty to work and the right to employment[8]. The operating logic is reversed, since the starting point is what people know, can do or want to do, and then they are mobilized by identifying what needs these skills can satisfy in the company's environment (on a territory). The experimentation is generating "undeniable enthusiasm" (Verkindt 2019) among local authorities. According to the TZCLD association, more than 200 local authorities are interested in joining the scheme. The scheme is awaiting the signing of a second law, which seems to be slow in coming because of the many doubts that surround the effectiveness of the experiment.

To summarize, all of the activities of the EOBs created in the 10 territories covered by the experiment mainly focus on market gardening, social link activities, services for individuals, services for businesses, building maintenance, recycling, lumbering and the maintaining of green spaces. In spite of the multiplication of their activities, the EOBs have an obligation to respect the initial objective of "supplementarity", i.e. activities that are not competitive with those already established on the territories. An analysis of these activities reveals that precariousness is their common characteristic, which in turn raises questions about the efficiency of the diffusion of the experimentation.

In addition to this precarity, other sources of doubt exist. First, the number of jobs created by the EOBs is far from sufficient for all of the long-term unemployed in the first 10 territories of the experiment. The Igas/IGF report notes the creation, up to June 2019, of 742 jobs in the EOBs, while there were more than 4,000 long-term unemployed in June 2018 in the 10 territories where the program is implemented[9]. "Even among the most advanced territories, none of them have yet been able to integrate the long-term unemployed who want to work" (Hédon et al. 2019, p. 286). This is why the

---

7 TZCLD Midterm Review 2019: http://etcld.fr/wp-content/uploads/2019/09/190926_ETCLD_bilan_LowRes.pdf (accessed: October 21, 2021).
8 See: https://www.legifrance.gouv.fr/Droit-francais/Constitution/Preambule-de-la-Constitution-du-27-Oct-1946 (accessed: October 21, 2021).
9 See: http://www.igas.gouv.fr/IMG/pdf/2019-050R.pdf (accessed: October 21, 2021).

Igas/IGF report recommends revising the eligibility criteria for people eligible to join the scheme, as well as reviewing the economic model of the experiment. Another concern (which is connected to the first) is the time frame of the project, which was initially planned to last for five years. This now seems to be insufficient: "It will take much more than five years for the first ten territories to achieve this" (Hédon et al. 2019, p. 287). All of these doubts point to the economic viability of the program. Its diffusion will be expensive, even more so than expected. According to the same report port by Igas/IGF, a full-time job in an EOB costs approximately EUR 26,000, whereas the initial estimate was EUR 18,000.

2.3.3. *A program in search of legitimacy*

The TZCLD experimentation is based on the implementation of a new form of entrepreneurship embodied by the EOBs. Indeed, the EOBs reverse the classical codes of functioning of traditional companies through principles such as non-selection and non-competition in a form of proto-institution, i.e. new practices that are closely tested in the 10 territories, and which may or may not progress to other stages. In addition to the benefits and the opportunity that the test moment can present, it also has an obvious and logical specificity, which is that of being limited in time. The TZCLD experimentation was started in November 2016 for a period of five years, and it has continued into 2021[10]. For this reason, the initiators of the TZCLD project are looking to give it a new lease on life and replicate it in between 50 and 100 new territories (Valentin 2018). The TZCLD association states that it has been contacted by more than 200 territories ready to implement the program.

The diffusion of the experiment to a larger number of territories testifies to the desire for the approach to gain legitimacy. One of the ways in which a practice is diffused is through institutional isomorphism, the key idea of which is to refer to institutionalized categories defined as superior (Strang and Meyer 1993). "Organizations not only compete for resources and customers, but are driven by the search for power and legitimacy" (Huault 2017, p. 172). The extension of the experimentation in itself embodies a recognition of its merits. However, the diffusion of the program to other territories is at a standstill and depends on the passage of a second law that

---

10 See: https://www.tzcld.fr/decouvrir-lexperimentation/les-territoires/ (accessed: October 21, 2021).

will authorize new territories to implement it, and new EOBs to be established. The Igas/IGF noted in its evaluation of the TZCLD project that the number of jobs created by the EOBs was not sufficient for all of the long-term unemployed identified in the experimental territories and that the planned costs for each job created were not controlled and have been exceeded.

These are some of the reasons why, in its latest report of October 2019, the Igas/IGF recommended that, before any temporal or geographical extension is adopted, the objectives and practical modalities of the experiment (beneficiary persons, EOB activities, mobilized funding) should be revised in order for the program to be able to achieve its original objectives. These recommendations represent an attempt to draw a general model from the first 10 territories, a sort of archetype that can be transposed to potential new territories. The aim is to formulate a theory of action that can be applied, because any theory raises the question of its effectiveness in practice. "A theory of a practice typically specifies the conditions necessary for its effective operation" (Strang and Meyer 1993, p. 497). The recommendations of the last Igas/IGF report and the delay in the vote on the second law are elements that have prompted the TZCLD association to set up a petition[11]. The aim is to collect signatures to accelerate the adoption of the second law and its vote. In other words, having failed to demonstrate social and economic efficiency in the light of the Igas/IGF report, we may wonder whether the TZCLD association is not just looking for another way to obtain legitimacy. Is it a proto-institution that will see its model spread and thus survive or will it end at the test stage and die?

2.4. Conclusion

According to the European Commission,

> social inclusion is a process that enables people at risk of poverty and social exclusion to participate in economic, social and cultural life and enjoy a decent standard of living. These people should be involved in the decision-making processes that affect their lives and can provide them better access to their fundamental rights (Bouquet 2015, p. 18).

---

11 See: https://www.change.org/p/richard-ferrand-pour-l-extension-de-l-expérimentation-territoires-zerounemployed-longterm?recruit=947230043&utm_source=share_petition&utm_medium=copylink&utm_campaign=share_petition (accessed: October 21, 2021).

The challenge facing organizations that adopt inclusive practices in their territories is to be a vehicle for social transformation in an environment that is characterized by economic, strategic and organizational constraints. In this regard, the system built to eradicate long-term unemployment in France is a rich source of information: it allows for the mobilization of the various stakeholders in a given territory, while at the same time proposing an approach for the diffusion of the experience from one territory to another.

2.5. References

Aldrich, H.E. and Fiol, C.M. (1994). Fools rush in the institutional context of industry creation. *The Academy of Management Review*, 19(4), 645–670.

Battilana, J., Leca, B., Boxenbaum, E. (2009). How actors change institutions: Towards a theory of institutional entrepreneurship. *Academy of Management Annals*, 3, 65–107.

Bauer, F. (2015). Inclusion et planification : vers un territoire inclusif. *Vie sociale*, 11(3), 71–80.

Berger, P.L. and Luckmann, T. (1967). *The Social Construction of Reality: A Treatise in the Sociology of Knowledge*. Anchor Books, New York.

Bouquet, B. (2015). L'inclusion : approche socio-sémantique. *Vie sociale*, 11(3), 15–25.

Bourdieu, P. (1997). *Les usages sociaux de la science. Pour une sociologie clinique du champ scientifique*. Éditions Quæ, Versailles.

Coleman, J.S. (1988). Social capital in the creation of human capital. *The American Journal of Sociology*, 94, 95–120.

Cummings, S., Bridgman, T., Hassard, J., Rowlinson, M. (2017). *A New History of Management*. Cambridge University Press, Cambridge.

Dansou, K. and Langley, A. (2012). Institutional work and the notion of test. *M@n@gement*, 15(5), 502–527.

DiMaggio, P.J. (1988). Interest and agency in institutional theory. In *Institutional Patterns and Organizations: Culture and Environment*, Zucker, L.G. (ed.). Ballinger, Cambridge.

DiMaggio, P.J. and Powell, W.W. (1983). The iron cage revisited: Institutional isomorphism and collective rationality in organizational fields. *American Sociological Review*, 48(2), 147–160.

DiMaggio, P.J. and Powell, W.W. (1991). Introduction. In *The New Institutionalism in Organizational Analysis*, Powell, W.W. and Dimaggio, P.J. (eds). University of Chicago Press, Chicago.

Ebersold, S. (2009). Inclusion. *Recherche et formation*, 61, 71–83.

Emirbayer, M. and Mische, A. (1998). What is agency? *The American Journal of Sociology*, 103(4), 962–1023.

Eynaud, P. and Mourey, D. (2015). Apports et limites de la production du chiffre dans l'entreprise sociale. Une étude de cas autour de la mesure de l'impact social. *Revue française de gestion*, 247, 85–100.

Fligstein, N. (1997). Social skill and institutional theory. *American Behavioral Scientist*, 40(4), 397–405.

Gardien, È. (2015). L'inclusion en pratiques : l'exemple de Jag, une ONG de personnes polyhandicapées vivant au cœur de la société suédoise. *Vie sociale*, 11(3), 81–95.

Gardou, C. (2012). *La société inclusive, parlons-en. Il n'y a pas de vie minuscule*. ERES, Toulouse.

Glémain, P. (2019). Un modèle de gestion sociale est-il envisageable ? *Gérer et comprendre*, 138(4), 57–58.

Godinot, X. (1995). *"On voudrait connaître le secret du travail". Dialogue insolite sur l'emploi entre militants du quart monde, chercheurs et acteurs de l'économie*. Les Éditions de l'Atelier, Paris.

Greenwood, R., Suddaby, R., Hinings, C.R. (2002). Theorizing change: The role of professional associations in the transformation of institutionalized fields. *Academy of Management Journal*, 45(1), 58–80.

Hédon, C., Goubert, D., Guillou, D.L. (2019). *Zéro chômeur : dix territoires relèvent le défi*. Les Éditions de l'Atelier, Paris.

Huault, I. (2008). Les approches critiques en management. In *Le management : fondements et renouvellements*, Schmidt, G. (ed.). Éditions Sciences Humaines, Auxerre.

Huault, I. (2017). Paul DiMaggio et Walter W. Powell, Des organisations en quête de légitimité. In *Les grands auteurs en management*, Charreire Petit, S. (ed.). EMS Editions, Caen.

Hwang, H. and Powell, W.W. (2005). Institutions and entrepreneurship. In *Handbook of Entrepreneurship Research*, Alvarez, S.A., Agarwal, R., Sorenson, O. (eds). Springer, New York.

Jepperson, R.L. (1991). Institutions, institutional effects, and institutionalism. In *The New Institutionalism in Organizational Analysis*, Powell, W.W. and DiMaggio, P.J. (eds). University of Chicago Press, Chicago.

Lawrence, T.B. (1999). Institutional strategy. *Journal of Management*, 25(2), 161–187.

Lawrence, T.B. and Suddaby, R. (2006). Institutions and institutional work. In *Handbook of Organization Studies*, Clegg, S.R., Hardy, C., Lawrence, T.B., Nord, W.R. (eds). Sage, London.

Lawrence, T.B., Hardy, C., Phillips, N. (2002). Institutional effects of interorganizational collaboration. The emergence of proto-institutions. *Academy of Management Journal*, 45(1), 281–290.

Lawrence, T.B., Suddaby, R., Leca, B. (2009). Introduction: Theorizing and studying institutional work. In *Institutional Work: Actors and Agency in Institutional Studies of Organizations*, Lawrence, T.B., Suddaby, R., Leca, B. (eds). Cambridge University Press, Cambridge.

Lawrence, T., Suddaby, R., Leca, B. (2011). Institutional work: Refocusing institutional studies of organization. *Journal of Management Inquiry*, 20(1), 52–58.

Luhmann, N. (1996). Membership and motives in social systems. *Systems Research*, 13(3), 341–348.

Maguire, S.B., Hardy, C.B., Lawrence, T.B. (2004). Institutional entrepreneurship in emerging fields. HIV/AIDS treatment advocacy in Canada. *Academy of Management Journal*, 47(5), 657–679.

Meyer, J.W. and Scott, R.W. (1983). *Organizational Environments: Ritual and Rationality*. London, Sage.

Ranger-Moore, J., Banaszak-Holl, J., Hannan, M.T. (1991). Density-dependent dynamics in regulated industries: Founding rates of banks and life insurance companies. *Administrative Science Quarterly*, 36(1), 36–65.

Rogers, E.M. (1962). Diffusion of innovations. *Revue française de sociologie*, 5-2, 216–218.

Selznick, P. (1949). *TVA and the Grass Roots: A Study in the Sociology of Formal Organization*. University of California Press, Berkeley.

Shore, L.M., Randel, A.E., Chung, B.G., Dean, M.A., Ehrhart, K.H., Singh, G. (2010). Inclusion and diversity in work groups: A review and model for future research. *Journal of Management*, 37(4), 1262–1289.

Strang, D. and Meyer, J.W. (1993). Institutional conditions for diffusion. *Theory and Society*, 22(4), 487–511.

Taupin, B. (2017). Thomas B., Lawrence et Roy Suddaby – Le travail institutionnel : le rôle des acteurs dans la relation institution organisation. In *Les grands auteurs en management*, Charreire Petit, S. (ed.). EMS Editions, Caen.

Valentin, P. (2013). Pour des territoires "zéro chômeur de longue durée". *Projet*, 336/337(5), 72–78.

Valentin, P. (2018). *Le droit d'obtenir un emploi : territoires zéro chômeur de longue durée. Genèse et mise en œuvre de l'expérimentation*. Chronique sociale, Lyon.

Verkindt, P.-Y. (2019). L'expérimentation "territoires zéro chômeur de longue durée". *Regards*, 56, 41–19.

3

The Inclusion of Lebanese Women with Breast Cancer: Between Stigma and Resilience

If the land of the cedars, where being beautiful remains a priority, benefits from a quality medical and plastic surgery infrastructure, it is because the Lebanese woman needs it to feel accepted by others, beauty or the physical aspect remaining a considerable asset in human relations. This is the context in which Lebanese women with breast cancer are fighting their battle. None of them can escape the pressures, the interactions that found and register their social ties and the social imaginary of the body with esthetic expectations related to physical appearance (Barkly 1990; Bordo 1993; Efrat 1995; Döring and Pöschl 2006), nor the representations that others have of women's symbolism, itself conditioned by a society with idealistic expectations (Bourdieu and Wacquant 2014). A woman with breast cancer must therefore fight her battle on several fronts: not only does she have to make a personal turnaround, but she also has to rely relentlessly on her inner strengths, her sense of duty and even on her femininity, which is undermined by the ruthless pathology. She must put her pragmatism at the service of her resilience to both convince her entourage directly and impose herself on her normative social environment, on the people in her own home, on her neighbors and, at work, on her colleagues, her partners and her bosses, who are often very compassionate, but who have been used to, since antiquity, shunning and labeling the disabled (Goffman 1975).

Chapter written by Nathalie CARIOU GHANTOUS, Jean-François CHANLAT and Laurence FROLOFF BROUCHE.

The question that arises is therefore whether today Lebanese society is ready to reintegrate female employees with breast cancer into the workplace, manage their skills, understand their diversity and ask itself the question of "living together" by taking into account the inequality and discrimination that these women face. In order to better understand this question, how the "damaged body", or the sick body (Le Breton 1991), is perceived, its involvement and its action in the context of Lebanese work, we conducted research in Lebanon with 25 women with breast cancer. Our study took place during their return to professional activity, which enabled us to better understand the conditions under which these women returned to work during treatment and the pitfalls they encountered in the business world. We first outline our theoretical framework, which draws upon three notions: social identity, stigmatization and resilience. Second, we detail our methodology and the approach we used for data collection. Finally, in the third part, we present the main results obtained from our research into the experience of illness at work in the Lebanese context.

3.1. From a social identity robbed by disease to stigmatization and resilience

To understand social representations of illness in the world of work, we must examine the convergence of the cycle of exchanges between the sick individual and the company where the coexistence of illness and work still practically does not exist: there are two options, we are either in good health or we are on sick leave. The world belongs to the healthy, and so does the professional sphere. Bringing illness into the workplace means bringing two opposing realities together. In the workplace, classifying labels (Tajfel and Turner 1985) can be seen as a way of re-establishing the norms of the organizational order (Chanlat 1990), since the health of employees represents an important material asset (Ashforth and Mael 1989). As these norms are changed by the presence of illness, as an attack on the body that disrupts the criteria of correspondence, we can observe the marginalization of the one who is labeled "sick" (Oaks and Turner 1980). Drawing on the work of Murray (2005), the concept of the body, which is experienced as "out of the ordinary", highlights the confused relationship between the physical and the psyche, as provoked by the glance of others. Thus, Mead (1934), Hoelter (1984) and Hayes and Ross (1986), among others, have highlighted the impact of negative judgments on workers experiencing illness and their impact on their self-esteem.

In our study, our participants also know that the physical and psychic transformations they have undergone, induced by the treatment of breast cancer, have disfigured them. The removal of their breast, the loss of their hair, the change in the color of their skin undermines the normative image of femininity and that of a "complete woman" (Owens 1993). The otherness entailed by these changes then becomes a vector of a degrading difference and cannot escape the gaze of others, who can tell that cancer has struck: the person feels diminished, stigmatized, discredited – their self-esteem is affected and their social identity shaken (Caron et al. 2007). In the context of work, this begs the following questions: To what extent will a woman with breast cancer, whose self-image has already been altered by invasive treatments, be stigmatized by the label of "cancer patient"? Will she suffer social exclusion or even face discrimination, which can lead to concrete forms of inequality? Employment is indeed a particularly favored area of observation for understanding the effects of the discriminations that result from judgments made about others because of these differences.

According to Goffman (1975), stigmatization is defined as a process that tends to discredit an individual who is considered to be "abnormal" by "normal" people. It involves a process of differentiation based on "labeling, categorization and stereotyping". Indeed, a person experiences stigma when they feel different because of a physical deformity that is suffered or innate. This physical attribute reduces them to being "contaminated" and "left out"; the stigma thus derives from an intimate situation. In contrast, Norbert Alter (2012) distinguishes the stigma of stigmatization from the fact that the stigma informs the stigmatization (the social process). It is a question of considering the modalities at work in stereotype construction, in the separation of labeled persons into distinct categories ("us" and "them"), in the disapproval, rejection and exclusion of people who are considered to be different.

Reintegrating employees with breast cancer back into the workplace and managing their skills are therefore perfectly in line with the spirit of this study. Integrating diversity within organizations means fostering the creation of a heterogeneous, complex team for greater efficiency and effectiveness and engendering more creativity and new ways of thinking (Barth and Falcoz 2008; Cornet and Warland 2008; Chanlat and Özbilgin 2018, 2019). Thinking about the link between diversity and difference also means establishing the ethics which supports it in a social project. It is in fact a vision of the company and of the human being who expresses themself based on socially responsible management.

This vision is shared in management studies by the movement associated with social and environmental responsibility (Mercier 2014; Brasseur 2016; Capron and Quairel-Lanoizelée 2016; Igalens and Gond 2018), i.e. the role that the company plays in a society and the anthropological issues associated with it (Chanlat 1990, 1998, 2012), including the relationship with the other, whether similar or different. Moreover, a reversal of stigmatization in the world of work cannot be achieved without the commitment of singular wills – such as in the case of the atypical bosses studied by Alter (2012), who showed that they reversed the process of stigmatization by finding strength in their difference. In light of these data and reflections, we wondered about the ability of our interviewees to bounce back: does work allow our sick employees a commitment that could reverse their destiny and rely on this strength that we call resilience?

Resilience is the art of bouncing back after a trauma, a shock or a hardship; it is also a capacity to live – to succeed and thrive in spite of any adversity (Cyrulnik and Jorland 2012). For some authors, following the example of Braconnier (1998), Vaillant (2000) and Michel Manciaux (2001), resilience is the result of the intensity of interactions that mobilize defense mechanisms in the subject concerned in response to the trauma they are experiencing. These defense mechanisms obviously depend on the degree of vulnerability of the person and their ability to solve their problems, which may be expressed by humor, sublimation or aggressiveness. Excluding the psychodynamic approaches of resilience, which give little room to the impact of our environment, we cannot speak of resilience without the existence of social interactions and external factors, as demonstrated by many researchers whose work dates back to the early 1990s (Rutter 1990; Garmezy 1991; Werner 1993), as well as more recent work, such as Cyrulnik and Jorland (2012) and Vanistendael (2006), who confirm the importance of social support systems (such as the family, community or society) in this process (Anaut 2005). Regardless of the etiquette attributed, will the Lebanese employee labeled with "breast cancer" be able, in light of these data, to gain respect for herself while undergoing treatment through the quality of her work and reverse the process of stigmatization into a strength? This is what our empirical study in Lebanon sought to understand.

3.2. The perspectives of 25 Lebanese women with breast cancer in the workplace

Our approach was intended to be qualitative, comprehensive and interpretative, in the sense that it focused on representing the points of view of the 25 women with breast cancer interviewed as they carried out their professional activity and understanding their individual experiences (Smith 2004; Reid et al. 2005), which amounts to replacing the notion of the sick body with that of the concrete disease. As such, we developed a semi-structured interview guide, which centered on three themes: (1) entry into the cycle of illness, the consequences of damage to the body regarding self-esteem and self-image, social representations of disease (prejudices and stereotypes); (2) the concordance of the work cycle in relation to the cycle of the illness (reintegration conditions, invalidity, management values); and (3) leaving the cycle with the recomposition and reconstruction of professional identity

The confidentiality and anonymity of the data collected were respected. We used Nvivo software to analyze the content of our findings. Of the 25 women interviewed, 21 were employees (11 executives and 10 employees) and 4 were business owners (1 of them also worked as a part-time university lecturer). At the time of the interviews, their average age was 46 years old, whereas their average age when their breast cancer was declared was 40 years old. More than half of our interviewees had worked for more than 13 years. Three of them worked in public sector companies and twenty-two in private sector companies. All but 1 of the interviewees (i.e. 24 out of 25) had undergone chemotherapy treatments. Two of the interviewees were in the relapse phase and twenty-three in remission. As such, our study focused on the perspectives of women in different phases of remission or relapse and on the difficulties that they faced in their respective workplaces.

3.2.1. *Beginning of the disease cycle and its representation in companies*

Having been unexpectedly affected by breast cancer during their career, weakened by the treatments (including surgery, chemotherapy, hormone therapy and radiotherapy) whose physical and psychological manifestations touched on their personal identity, by losing their breasts, our 25 interviewees had all experienced the loss of the symbol of their femininity, a stigma that would stay with them for life. Their self-image was deeply affected. Less beautiful, they perceived themselves as having become other: changed, diminished, humiliated by baldness and deformations of their bodies (some experienced excessive weight gain, whereas others suffered from second-degree burns as a result of radiotherapy, etc.). The lymph node removal that often accompanies ablation surgery of the breast, when it takes place, can also lead to disabling effects on the arm, such as lymphedema and big arm syndrome, which requires a fairly long convalescence before the limb can be fully mobile again. In addition to this, there is psychological suffering, including a kind of fear around identity and gender which negatively affects their self-esteem and self-confidence.

Troubled by a feeling of inferiority and fear of no longer being accepted due to sexual nonconformity, often forced to undergo the removal of other gynecological organs (such as the uterus, fallopian tubes and ovaries) that may be related to their primary breast cancer, some experienced separations and relationship breakdowns, whereas others experienced suicidal thoughts related to feelings of guilt and abandonment. Faced with the specter of death, most of them try to smile normally, to spare the suffering of the people who love them and who, for the most part, accompany them thanks to the traditional Lebanese way of life that favors "living together". It is according to the nature of their relationship, intimate or indifferent, with their entourage that our interviewees decide in front of whom to let their illness appear. About 20 of them hide it, especially when the nature of certain professions requires it; in these cases, the profession of insurance broker responsible for guaranteeing lives, or that of the manager of a large hotel in Beirut who has to welcome clients all day long, or that of the medical assistant of a plastic surgeon where physical appearance is paramount, or that of the personal assistant of a boss in the luxury industry who is supposed to convey the brand image that the company represents.

Others had to even more carefully decipher the gaze of others, which remains hurtful. The wig and the physical changes caused by chemotherapy mean that those around them cannot ignore that cancer has struck. Pitying or encouraging, indelicate or disdainful or even hostile, the eye of the boss, the colleague, or the well-heeled client reminds them that their stigma is there and that they cannot escape it:

> "Other people come to you and say, "oh, you have cancer!"" (interviewee 7); "The look in people's eyes kills me, they look at you in a way. Oh, poor thing, oh... She looks... I don't like... I don't like being looked at with pity" (interviewee 25); "People want to see the sick person in their own way... They're the ones who feel bad... People are not nice! They don't want to see us like this!... And my colleagues wanted me to wear it (the wig), they felt better when I put it on" (interviewee 18).

3.2.2. *Work cycle, illness cycle: concordances*

The interviews that we collected over the course of our research illustrate the role of context in personal and social stigma (at work and at home). By describing concretely convergent experiences in their reality, our interviewees bring us back to things as they are, with the urgency leaving very little room for introspection. The first thing that these women felt was guilt and shame, and they sought to isolate themselves, to stay away from the public eye, because they felt so inadequate that they doubted their own worth. They found it normal for others to have difficulty accepting their state of difference because they knew that the workplace would not tolerate either breaches of presentation or nonconformity. Having experienced alienation in their social lives (abandonment and separation), stigmatization at work felt as harsh as it was painful and affected their professional identity. Marginalized, categorized, automatically labeled by illness and the mandatory health check-up upon hiring, and therefore assumed to be less efficient, our interviewees have had to live through criticism, reprimands and humiliating remarks:

> "People are shocked by the sight of a bald woman. It isn't common, the woman is labeled affected, it is the look of others that makes me feel this [...]. Even with the scarf people complimented me that it looked good on me and when I turned my back I heard them say: "The poor girl has cancer"" (interviewee 5); "Being labelled because of the disease is very real and I confronted a newly hired higher-up colleague who had recently mentioned my disease as the reason for a decrease

in productivity. This bothered me a lot and I had to speak up" (interviewee 2); "At the beginning, people are very compassionate towards cancer patients, but with time and as the treatment is long [...] we're no longer seen, the concern for productivity prevails" (interviewee 10); "At the beginning, when I learned about my illness, I'd approached the director of care. I told her that I was going to have to take time off work [...]. She was very receptive [...] after my second surgery (because after my breast removal, I had to have an oophorectomy) [...] they told me that I had to come back or they'd deduct my salary [...]. And my annual leave counted for my time off" (interviewee 23).

As far as management is concerned, there is a before and after, a beginning and an end, as if, after having behaved humanely at first when the illness was announced, they lost patience and became hardened to practice all kinds of discrimination. For the sake of productivity and financial performance, the boss focuses on their own interests, while human resources are more interested in the workers as a production machine, something that determines the health of the company, than as human beings. In fact, our study shed light on various ways to push workers experiencing illnesses to resign, including depriving them of rights, issuing penalties for work stoppages, reductions of salaries or refusals of salary increases, demotions and discounting of bonuses and annual leave, not to mention dismissals, moral harassment, verbal violence and psychological pressure.

At the end of our survey, only 15 of the 25 women interviewed were still in their jobs. Of these 15, only 3 were employed in the public sector, 4 were business owners and 2 were at the end of their lives. In return for remaining in the company, some of them accepted internal arrangements: 3 out of the 25 were demoted and 7 out of the 25 who had not kept the same job have since had to leave it (5 of these 7 people were forced to resign and 2 were dismissed).

The intersection of the concepts "discrimination" and "management" highlights the strong links that exist at work between discrimination and non-equitable management. It also justifies the non-existence of discrimination at work when management acts fairly. While they are stigmatized because of their illness, they also face other discriminations from outside the workplace – from insurance, social security and the Ministry of

Public Health – which accumulate, with banks further complicating this bleak picture of injustice. The Lebanese cancer patient has to live with these inequalities, sometimes on her own account, and suffer the consequences of a social burden that weighs as much as the disease itself. If any employer who offers an employment contract to their employee is obliged in Lebanon to subscribe to social security, they can also offer them a group mutual insurance at quite interesting group rates covering the difference that the social security refuses to pay.

However, it is important to add that social security only provides patients with social protection for up to 90% of the full hospital coverage and 80% of the medical consultations and prescribed drugs. It is also important to note that the National Social Security Fund (NSSF/CNSS) reimbursement for certain imaging procedures, genetic tests, radiotherapy, etc., is not guaranteed to be 100%: the social security only reimburses 80% of the expenses, considered on the basis of its own tariffs, which were established long ago and are still in force, and are far lower than the real tariffs set by hospitals and imaging centers, so that the patient is forced to pay the difference, or even, in some cases, the entire amount.

Moreover, when an employee loses their job, they also lose their social security rights after three months. However, they can register for self-employed welfare benefits and benefit from the same rights as those mentioned above. As far as mutual insurance companies are concerned, the clauses do not always cover the expenses incurred. For example, some business owners who are not entitled to social security (being a business owner and not a salaried employee) found themselves excluded from mutual insurance companies the following year, while still undergoing expensive post-treatment, and suffering from the restrictions on coverage for cancer cases in general. Therefore, in order to keep their mutual insurance, they are subjected to higher rates, which far exceed the normal rates which they used to pay before their illness, since they now carry the restricting label of "sick". Finally, it should be pointed out that in case of loss of employment, the employee also loses their mutual insurance if the clause concerning the "renewal guarantee" was not formally stipulated at the signing of the membership contract. This leads to many cases of litigation over the refusal of insurance companies to cover cancer patients under the pretext that their treatments have become too expensive.

As we can see, the burden of cancer is thus not limited to the disease itself, but to the health coverage system as a whole, and, in particular, to treatments that are out of reach to the average person. The employee who loses their job will have only one choice: to turn to the banks for a personal loan. However, here again, discrimination can be very present: banks categorically refuse to grant loans to cancer patients. Since life insurance is, for all intents and purposes, not an option for them, they have only one option left: to return to the public health system, as the Ministry of Public Health is responsible for insuring every Lebanese citizen free of charge. However, this remains problematic, as private hospitals, which are obliged to be well managed in order to ensure the functioning and profitability of their facilities, impose a very limited intake quota on patients covered by the Ministry due to the long delays in the reimbursement of care by the public sector.

3.2.3. *Resilience and trajectories*

At the end of this rollercoaster ride, we observed that all the interviewees had a form of resilience in order to overcome their trauma, our 25 interviewees having drawn their energy to live from this struggle, which they also saw as a struggle for love; in some cases, it was perhaps a matter of protecting their loved ones, whom they felt responsible for. In terms of "give and take", they first received positive support from those around them, from which some of them drew their courage. Having become strong in their difference, they took up the challenge of not altering anything in their productivity. Far from what we might think, it is not a return to employment that they are facing because they have never left it. By taking refuge in it, work becomes a source of healing; it makes them forget the illness, keeps them busy and gives them hope.

Although surgery and chemotherapy require them to take time off work, many of them are more eager to improve their performance than their healthy colleagues and, in overcoming their physical weaknesses, are more productive. Anticipating their downtime, we have seen them return to work postoperatively, equipped with their drains, despite having stitches in unhealed wounds. They and their siblings have been known to go to chemotherapy on Fridays, thus saving their weekends so that their performance is not affected in any way. In the case of radiotherapy, they prefer not to take time off work and admit that they have suffered the effects of the treatment (burns and other after-effects) and yet returned to work the same day. Certain hospital schedules are even arranged for these workers. On days when our interviewees were absent due to treatment, they continued to work at home. To maintain their position, they paid more attention to detail and were more efficient and more committed. They took pride in never having left anything unfinished. As their bodies were being affected by the disease, none of them hesitated to have their bodies reconstructed in one way or another (by wearing different styles and colors of wigs, scarves, hats or caps according to their own taste, ysing make-up and tattoos, changing their clothing style and coquetterie, breast reconstructions). In order to sublimate their sorrows, the fear of the absurdity of their situation, and to rebuild themselves psychologically, a strange force develops thanks to the laughter, some breaking the social codes with nonconformist behavior, eccentric and exhibitionist. These people now live under the threat of relapse, their attitudes manifesting a change in the order of priorities where their health and personal well-being now take precedence.

As far as their resilience is concerned, although we found a number of points of convergence with the work of Michel Manciaux (2001), Stéfan Vanistendael (2006) and Boris Cyrulnik (2017), we were forced to note that, in their case, an openly displayed belief in the divine power emerged from our data; this demonstrates a strong relationship between resilience and degree of religiosity. In their case, praying gave them the strength to fight; a supernatural strength from prayer helped them to overcome the torments of the disease and to continue living. Their illness becomes a test, willed by God, who they view as their protector and, if they wish, their healer. Whatever their religion, they are not afraid to identify themselves with holiness, as the martyrs claim, and seek to transmit a message of faith to their fellow humans:

> "I'm of a strong character, I'm resilient and I draw my strength from God. Life is full of problems, we must not give up, we must continue our way of the cross" (interviewee 22); "Whatever difficulties life brings, you can protect yourself. You have to have faith. Faith protects you from everything. Faith in God… That's what I think. You go through a lot of trials in a lifetime. God puts a lot of things in your way. For me, they are challenges. Each time you overcome one, he will send you another one, more difficult, and always to make you strong, to

strengthen your faith" (interviewee 24); "The relationship with God changes, I think, because I almost died and I came back. God brought me back to life. The Blessed Virgin also did not leave me. My operation lasted 7 hours, thanks to God, he is my protector" (interviewee 13).

Furthermore, in reference to Alter's (2012) concept of "passing/passer" and social commitment, we can see them put their shift in the service of a responsible engagement in order to fight against the disease. Guided by a sense of empathy, they understand, help, support, listen to, advise and encourage other patients: their understanding is a sharing of experience that is irreplaceable. Through their presence and their words, they become the mediators of their fellow human beings.

3.3. Conclusion

This study sought to highlight the characteristics of a body damaged by the effects of physical and psychological transformations induced by the treatment of breast cancer and their influence on the social identity and self-esteem of women who suffer from it in Lebanon. The research was spread over approximately 18 months during which time the women affected were professionally active and beginning to reintegrate into the world of work. The examination of "marks of cancer" refers to Goffman's (1975) approach to the stigmatization of "labels" and the social representations that derive from it. As we have seen, the reality of the lived sick body is projected in the gaze of others, which is not without an effect on the relationship with oneself and with others. The gaze of the other always comes to remind us that the stereotypes are there and that we cannot escape them. Otherness, in this case disease, becomes a vector of a degrading difference and the affected person is diminished in the eyes of those around them.

As such, our results and analysis join the work of Alter (2012) on "atypical" patterns, where he showed how the stages of an exclusion process can also be transformed into resources for inclusion. In our case, our interviews revealed that this transformation – i.e. this conversion of a physical and apparent stigma into an individual will – allowed a form of integration despite all the obstacles encountered. Indeed, such was the case for these women suffering from breast cancer in the workplace; despite the intimate and social stigmatization, as well as the discrimination suffered on a daily basis, they never gave up. Instead, they showed that they were more committed, more attentive to the smallest details, and capable of overcoming these challenges and reversing their social destiny by converting their differences into strength. In some cases, their resilience was found to lead to higher productivity. In solidarity with their peers, they did not hesitate to advise, support, help and inform, aiming to improve the prognosis of the disease and their chance of survival. Finally, since our work has focused solely on the Lebanese context, it would be interesting to extend the analysis to eventually produce a more detailed and more representative comparison of the private and public sectors. It would also be interesting to later be able to complement it with more research on managerial practices and mechanisms for greater social inclusion.

3.4. References

Alter, N. (2012). *La force de la différence. Itinéraires de patrons atypiques.* PUF, Paris.

Anaut, M. (2005). Le concept de résilience et ses applications cliniques. *Recherche en soins infirmiers*, 82, 4–11.

Ashforth, B. and Mael, F. (1989). Social identity theory and the organization. *Academy of Management Review*, 14(1), 20–39.

Barkly, S. (1990). *Feminity and Domination: Studies in the Phenomenology of Oppression.* Routledge, New York.

Barth, I. and Falcoz, C. (2008). *Le management de la diversité. Enjeux, fondements et pratiques.* L'Harmattan, Paris.

Bordo, S. (1993). *Unbearable Weight: Feminism, Western Culture and the Body.* University of California Press, Berkeley.

Bourdieu, P. and Wacquant, L. (2014). *Invitation à la sociologie réflexive.* Le Seuil, Paris.

Braconnier, A. (1998). *Psychologie dynamique et psychanalyse.* Masson, Paris.

Brasseur, M. (2016). *L'Éthique et l'entreprise.* L'Harmattan, Paris.

Capron, M. and Quairel-Lanoizelée, F. (2016). *La responsabilité sociale d'entreprise.* La Découverte, Paris.

Caron, R., Leroy, F., Berl, S., Beaune, D. (2007). L'impossible écart entre représentations du corps malade et représentation de soi. *Psycho-oncologie*, 1, 41–47.

Chanlat, J.F. (1990). *L'individu dans l'organisation. Les dimensions oubliées*. Eska, Paris.

Chanlat, J.F. (1998). *Sciences sociales et management. Plaidoyer pour une anthropologie générale*. Les Presses de l'université Laval, Quebec.

Chanlat, J.F. (2012). Anthropologie des organisations. In *Encyclopédie des Ressources Humaines*, Allouche, J. (ed.). Vuibert, Paris.

Chanlat, J.F. and Özbilgin, M. (2018). *Management et diversité. Tome 1 : Comparaisons internationales*. Les Presses de l'université Laval, Quebec.

Chanlat, J.F. and Özbilgin, M. (2019). *Management et diversité. Tome 2 : Approches thématiques, enjeux et défis sociopolitiques*. Les Presses de l'université Laval, Quebec.

Cornet, A. and Warland, P. (2008). *GRH et gestion de la diversité*. Dunod, Paris.

Cyrulnik, B. (2017). *Psychothérapie, de Dieu*. Odile Jacob, Paris.

Cyrulnik, B. and Jorland, J. (2012). *Résilience connaissance de base*. Odile Jacob, Paris.

Döring, N. and Pöschl, S. (2006). Images of men and women in mobile phone advertisements: A content analysis of advertisements for mobile communication systems. *Sex Symbols*, 55, 173–185.

Efrat, T. (1995). *The Masque of Feminity. The Presentation of Woman in Everyday Life*. Sage, London.

Garmezy, N. (1991). Resilience in children's adaptation to negative life events and stressed environments. *Pediatric*, 20(9), 459–460.

Goffman, E. (1975). *Stigmate. Les usages sociaux des handicaps*. Les Éditions de Minuit, Paris.

Hayes, D. and Ross, C.E. (1986). Body and mind: The effect of exercise, overweight, and physical health on psychological well-being. *Journal of Health and Social Behavior*, 27(4), 387–400.

Hoelter, J.W. (1984). Relative effects of significant others on self-evaluation. *Social Psychology Quarterly*, 47(3), 255–262.

Igalens, J. and Gond, J.P. (2018). *La responsabilité sociale de l'entreprise*. PUF, Paris.

Le Breton, D. (1991). Sociologie du corps : perspective. *Cahiers internationaux de sociologie*, 90, 131–143.

Manciaux, M. (2001). La résilience. Un regard qui fait vivre. *Études*, 395, 321–330.

Mead, G.H. (1934). *Mind, Self and Society from the Standpoint of a Social Behaviorist: The Works of George Herbert Mead*. University of Chicago Press, Chicago.

Mercier, S. (2014). *L'éthique dans les entreprises*. La Découverte, Paris.

Murray, S. (2005). Doing politics or selling out? Living the fat body. *Women's Studies*, 34(3), 265–277.

Oaks, P.J. and Turner, J.C. (1980). Social categorization and intergroup behaviour: Does minimal intergroup discrimination make social identity more positive? *European Journal of Social Psychology*, 10, 295–301.

Owens, T.J. (1993). Accentuate the positive and the negative: Rethinking the use of self-esteem, self-depreciation, and self-confidence. *Social Psychology Quarterly*, 56, 288–299.

Reid, K., Flowers, P., Larkin, M. (2005). Interpretative phenomenological analysis: An overview and methodological review. *The Psychologist*, 18, 20–23.

Rutter, M. (1990). Psychosocial resilience and protective mechanisms. In *Risk and Protective Factors in the Development of Psychopathology*, Rolf, J., Masten, A.S., Cicchetti, D., Nuechterlein, K.H., Weintraub, S. (eds). Cambridge University Press, New York.

Smith, J.A. (2004). Reflecting on the development of interpretative phenomenological analysis and its contribution to qualitative research in psychology. *Qualitative Research in Psychology*, 1, 39–54.

Tajfel, H. and Turner, J.C. (1985). The social identity theory of intergroup behavior. In *Psychology of Intergroup Relations*, Worchel, S. and Austin, W.G. (eds). Nelson Hall Publishers, London.

Vaillant, G.E. (2000). *The Wisdom of the Ego*. Harvard University Press, Cambridge.

Vanistendael, S. (2006). *La résilience ou le réalisme de l'espérance : blessé mais pas vaincu*. Cahiers du BICE, Geneva.

Werner, E. (1993). What can we learn about resilience from large scale longitudinal studies? In *Handbook of Resilience in Children*, Goldstein, S. and Brooks, R.B. (eds). Springer, New York.

4

Women Entrepreneurs from Deprived Areas as Generators of Inclusion: A Capabilities Interpretation

This chapter examines women's entrepreneurship as a driving force for territorial inclusion. We seek to underline the following issue: how can women's entrepreneurship in deprived areas or neighborhoods (*quartiers dits politique de la ville* (QPVs)) generate inclusion in a territory? To answer this question, we start with a summary of the state of the art on inclusive territories that we cross-reference with the work of Sen to construct a grid for reading such territories based on capabilities. We use this grid in order to understand the individual, environmental and social conversion factors in the representations of women who wish to be involved in entrepreneurship.

We met all these women during a training course dedicated to social entrepreneurship in the "Cité des 4000" in La Courneuve, which symbolizes deprived areas, in the northern suburbs of Paris. We retrace their experiences on their path to entrepreneurship. By following the trajectories of these entrepreneurs and what they are becoming, it is possible to highlight the importance of the spatial variable in the entrepreneurial project. The results led us to consider the relationship between women and their environment from the perspective of capabilities. The discussion proposes an understanding of entrepreneurship as a tool to serve an inclusive territory. It highlights a positive spiral that is part of the dynamic of co-constructing the territory and entrepreneurship.

Chapter written by Amélie NOTAIS and Julie TIXIER.

4.1. Proposition of a framework for analyzing the inclusive territory

We present the notion of inclusive territory before proposing an interpretation grid based on Sen's concept of capabilities (1992).

4.1.1. *Inclusive territory: a fuzzy target*

The concept of a territory is widely used in various disciplines, including in economics and geography. However, its rough edges are quickly revealed. Thus, linking territory and inclusion is a challenge. Geographers have been studying territory for many years. The work of Lévy and Lussault (2003) separates space and territory on the basis of historical specificities and the identity imprint that shapes the territory. Di Méo (2011) emphasizes the extent to which inhabitants shape and construct this living space and make it the scene of interactions with the environment. This bounded and controlled space that is the territory is marked by the users who construct it day-to-day: "For there to be a territory, three proximities must be combined: spatial, organizational and institutional" (Colletis et al. 2005, p. 296). This research from the field of economic geography encourages us to understand a territory beyond mere spatial proximity and underlines the complexity of the delimitation of the territory as a result of the entanglement of multiple proximal dimensions within it.

Bouchard et al. (2007) identify five main types of territory: societal, reticular, physical, administrative and action. The "social or societal territory" integrates the social link, the identities of the population, in the relationship to space. The "reticular territory" relates to the networking of actors. The "physical territory" refers to the elements of a territory that are related to nature, the environment or infrastructure. The "administrative territory" refers to the institutional territory of economic geography. The "territory of production of action" considers the territory to be the basis of collective actions carried out through the identity of the actors. These five types of territory are intertwined and complement each other. They constitute an important element of analysis in our research, in the sense that territory influences action and represents opportunities for as well as obstacles to women's entrepreneurship. The context of deprived areas, still little studied today, presents specific features in terms of women's opportunities for action. From Bouchard et al.'s (2007) typology, we both retain the complexity of the five types of territory and pay particular attention to the territory that produces action, whose indicators include the territorial anchoring of organizations and companies, and the creation and maintenance of employment.

Pecqueur, in 2009, justified the ambiguity of the concept of territory because of the various translations of the term *territory* into French as an instituted territory and a "place" as constructed by the actors. He also questioned the notion of proximity, which is often presented as a feature of a territory, and shows how this proximity encloses and "creates community" and can even generate conflict. Territory appears to be a complex and protean concept. The notion of proximity is central, but its performativity is challenged. Territory and its different meanings underline the importance of both spatial and social contextualization of research. The multiplicity of territories and their entanglements make it difficult to clearly delimit a territory. The previous research of geographers invites us to question the way in which they are inhabited. The multiple and reciprocal interactions between the actors and a territory build a perpetual dynamic of evolution of its contours. It is within this dynamic and malleable territory that the issues of inclusion are articulated.

4.1.2. *Generating inclusion: from concept to action*

According to the European Commission,

> social inclusion is a process that ensures that people at risk of poverty or exclusion obtain the opportunities and resources necessary to be able to fully participate fully in economic, social and cultural life, and that they enjoy a standard of living and well-being considered normal for the society in which they live. Social inclusion guarantees them better participation in the decision-making processes that affect their lives and better access to their fundamental rights (European Commission communication from 12 December 2003).

Social inclusion is both a state of living standards and a process of participation in the decisions that create society. However, Puaud (2019) points to the "indefinition" of the term, which has been denounced for being either a "catch-all" term that ignores "the root causes of social and economic inequalities" or for its foundations based on dissymmetry since "it is the powerful that decide whether or not to include a dominated group" (Clerc and Deboulet 2018). As such, social inclusion remains a vague concept.

Bauer (2015) calls for a transdisciplinary approach to address these challenges raised by social inclusion. He highlights the richness of this notion of social inclusion as an "ideal horizon", since it is both a static and dynamic concept. However, inclusion is also

> definable as a process, implying consequent work of society on itself [...]. More than a concept of social adjustment and compensation, the concept of inclusion must be understood and used as a general and fundamental societal project, concerning, in its implementation as well as in its results, all citizens (Bauer 2015, pp. 72–73).

Clément and Valegeas (2017) characterize the replacement of the term "diversity" as a "mobilizing myth" with the term "inclusion" in city policy discourses. They explain that the successful dissemination and appropriation of the concept of inclusion is due to the volatility of its content: according to them, the inclusive city denotes a utopia whose conditions of emergence remain unclear and little questioned.

Definitions of the inclusive city all emphasize the need for a participatory and democratic process that is inherent to inclusion. While a city's institutions can become more open and adopt a participatory approach, the territory, by contrast, with its vague contours and multiple dimensions, strikes us as difficult to make participatory. The modalities for setting up a demographic and participatory dimension on the scale of the territory must be questioned. The literature emphasizes the role of institutions in the development and emergence of this participatory process. For us, the inhabitants' potential for action in a territory is an element that needs to be examined further. To this end, we have found the literature on capabilities to be particularly enlightening. There is a certain consensus around the definition of inclusion as put forward by the Nobel Prize winner in economics, Amartya Sen: "Inclusion is characterized by the widely shared social experience and active participation of a society, by the generalized equality of opportunities and life chances available to people at the individual level, and by the attainment of a basic level of well-being for all citizens" (Sen 1992).

Inclusion necessarily leads to questions related to social justice and inequality. In this sense, Puaud (2019) questions the notion of margins in an inclusive society by quoting Tuot, who declared:

> I propose we move towards an inclusive society, in which no one would be on the margins, nor especially on the other side of the margins [...] The foreign dimension would not be denied, but it would no longer be the major explanatory variable of social difficulties. The way to achieve this could be what the Americans call *empowerment*, which I have translated as "*mise en capacité*" [capacity setting] (Tuot 2013 in Puaud 2019, p. 4).

By combining inclusion and empowerment, Puaud sees people as owing it to themselves to be inclusive. It is in this sense that we make use of the notion of capabilities in order to analyze the capacity of individuals to act within a territory, to mobilize their resources and to transform perceived opportunities into action on their territory.

Sen (1992, pp. 12–13 and p. 29) employed the term "capabilities" to express "all the modes of human functioning that are potentially accessible to a person, whether or not he or she exercises them". These modes are "the opportunities that an individual has to achieve his or her objectives". Capabilities refer to the possibility for individuals to make choices among the goods that they consider valuable and to effectively achieve them. Capabilities therefore refer to the functioning (what I do), the resources (what I have) and the conversion factors (individual, social and environmental) that facilitate the real issues of social justice and human well-being. These conversion factors are mobilized as operational descriptors for reading the data collected and understanding the diversity of spaces perceived by individuals.

4.2. A qualitative and sensitive approach to local women's entrepreneurship

Since 2013, a qualitative methodology has been deployed during the observation of social entrepreneurship training sessions in the heart of the Cité des 4000 in La Courneuve. Each year, for one week, about 40 women are trained in social entrepreneurship, with the aim of creating their own businesses and, in most cases, their jobs. In 2013, the first training session was held and provided us with the opportunity to meet six of the women and two to three women entrepreneurs in each of the following sessions. In total, the study followed the paths of 19 of the women.

	2013	2014	2015	2016	2017
Interviews	Six women	Four women	Three women	Two women	Four women
Follow-up interviews	–		Interviews with some of the women met in previous years (collection beyond 2017)		
Observations and meetings		Follow-up of the training			
		Graduation			
		Meetings with some members of the association			
Photos		–	Portraits of women and posters presenting their project		
			Photos of collective moments		
		–		Photos of the work spaces and surroundings of the training (public space)	
Videos	–	–	Filmed interviews as well as collective moments (training and breaks)		–

Table 4.1. *The various methods of data collection deployed from 2013 to 2017*

The first interviews were organized on the sidelines of the training sessions. In these interviews, each of the women was invited to talk about her project in the form of a life story (Bertaux 1997), focusing on the role of the training, the obstacles she had faced and the driving forces behind its success. The follow-up interviews aimed to build on the elements highlighted. They were personalized to better grasp the pathway towards the creation of a company for each of the women entrepreneurs. In addition to the interviews, numerous photos and videos were collected during the training sessions in order to capture the collective spirit of each of the sessions. For a week, the training session took place in one of the participants' living spaces. The variety of data collected (Table 4.1) and our logbooks took our approach further. We added feelings and affects to the raw data in order to express this field of study with very fine granularity in a spatial and temporal approach. Vulbeau (2007) suggests this approach in order to capture a certain richness, whether in individuals or in territories. According to the author, "it is also the space to which one must be sensitive, humanly speaking, in order to hear its singularities and enhance its potential" (Vulbeau 2007, p. 12). As such, he invites the researcher to move closer and to favor "a scale of observation attentive to what is perceptible by the senses".

Our methodology sought to capture the power of the action perceived by actors in their territory, the capabilities of the inhabitants in their territory and their perceptions of the conversion factors. We did not adopt a traditional approach rooted in an economic rationality of capabilities, which translates human behaviors into an equation. Instead, we adopted a more flexible approach, which took into account the importance of the effect of the environment on the possibilities of action of individuals. By employing this loose approach, our aim was to understand capabilities in relation to the space in which they are embedded. We used conversion factors as operational descriptors to code and then analyze the stories of women:

1) Environmental conversion factors are the perceived opportunities of the environment. The infrastructures that support entrepreneurship include the association that organizes the training week in partnership with the social incubator of a major French business school and public aid intended to promote women's entrepreneurship and entrepreneurship in the neighborhoods, for example, or aid at the level of the collectives registered on the territory (associations, networks, etc.).

2) Social conversion factors refer to the women's own perception of the possibility for them to become entrepreneurs in reality. We analyze the cultural and social aspects framing entrepreneurship and, in particular, gender norms.

3) Individual conversion factors concern the perception of the skills and capacities of the woman herself. This refers to the women's own feelings of being ready to take action and become fully entrepreneurial.

The reading grid provided by the capabilities approach highlights women's relationship with the territory, their capabilities and the conversion factors (environmental, social and individual). We used it to code all the interviews. To better understand the specificities of the challenges faced by these women and to report on them in an embodied way, we scatter the presentation of the results with illustrative quotations without claiming to generalize. We sought, on the contrary, to explore the richness and diversity of entrepreneurial trajectories by highlighting certain patterns.

4.3. The capabilities of women entrepreneurs: a potential tool for inclusion

In this section, we present an approach to women's capabilities by detailing the environmental, social and individual conversion factors.

4.3.1. *Environmental conversion factors*

First and foremost, the failings of the environment represent an anthill of entrepreneurial ideas. The daily environment, where these women watch their children grow up, is a generator of entrepreneurial ideas. In fact, the business ideas and projects of all the women we met were born out of the shortcomings they faced. Very often, the answer to their problems (which they sometimes faced on a daily basis) was totally absent; the French State did not take them on board or only did so to a limited extent, and some of these problems remained under the radar of the policies in these deprived areas. In deprived areas, the environment can appear to be hostile due to the lack of infrastructure related to economic development and entrepreneurship. However, for some of the women, this lack of infrastructure and these shortcomings represented entrepreneurial opportunities. This was the case for Hafida, who designed an application that would allow social housing associations to better communicate with their tenants. As she explained,

> I see my dad on his tablet [...] I see that he manages to answer [the traffic code questions] despite the text and the spoken parts [my dad is illiterate and has only 10% of his hearing ability]. I see this and I say to myself: I want to do something in the digital world [...] We'll allow rental life to be healthier, or in any case, provide a better environment to live together in the same place, share and respect the needs of others, and [...] perhaps tenants who do not master the language will be able to communicate since I imagine the application with pictograms (Hafida).

All of the women spoke of the daily environment as a paradoxically fertile ground despite the problems of discrimination, insecurity, poverty and difficulties accessing culture or even the most basic healthcare.

Training also emerged as a factor in the conversion of the environment. The training program is co-financed by a French business school, the Île-de-France region, a city contract, the European Social Fund (as part of the social component of Greater Paris) and a private company. It was offered to women from deprived areas with a social entrepreneurship project. The facilitators provide six days of training in social entrepreneurship and help the women to develop their projects. The objective of the training is to transform this abundance of ideas into real business projects. It is a real factor of conversion of the environment and allows some women to nourish new hopes, both in terms of their individual perspectives and in terms of the evolution of their environment.

Fatma's story is a good illustration of the tensions and hopes of the business project. Fatma was forced to close down her bakery (which had been located in a difficult neighborhood) after experiencing several robberies, competition from hypermarkets and the closure of numerous other local businesses. Today, she wants to try again; she sees that new businesses are opening in her neighborhood. She also notes bitterly: "My children do not work… They do not want to work elsewhere. My husband doesn't work." Even though she admits that she is not perfectly safe in this area, she does not want to move her establishment elsewhere: "I'm staying anyway." This job, for her and her entire family, is also a way to stay on the right path: the training helps her to refine her project and business plan, and above all, work out how to link her business to her heritage by including Algerian pastries into what is a traditional French bakery. Training is one of the structuring infrastructures of the environment for these women, which many of them refer to as a real "booster" for their ideas.

4.3.2. *Social conversion factors*

Training also seems to represent a social conversion factor. The energy that emerges from each of the training sessions is particularly strong. In each of them, new projects emerge, associating two participants according to their affinities. However, when we see the women who are left out of the training, many of them are disappointed and bitter – while the training gave them an impetus, it was not sustained over time. The wind has been taken out of their sails. For their part, the members of the organization explained to us that their mission ends there and that they do not have the financial and human resources to accompany the women beyond that point (their funding was initially only intended for the preterm phase).

The solitude of the entrepreneurial journey was overcome by some women who, in addition to the training sessions, decided to meet once a month. They organized themselves and met up in each other's homes to help each other progress. For them, this collective dynamic, which stemmed from the training, was indispensable in helping their respective projects succeed. The follow-up of the actions of the association allowed us to note the importance conferred to social interactions. The association has sought new subsidies and has thus been able to modify the scope of its action. Its offer has progressively integrated collective intelligence workshops to meet this emerging need. Entrepreneurship training for women is a social conversion factor that enables women to get started. This week of training crystallizes the drivers and elements that support them in their project. It favors and even precipitates the action of taking. At the same time, women were questioning their ability to become entrepreneurs.

Associating women and entrepreneurship, each one of them refers to the singularity of her path. For some, like Marie, it was a matter of putting a name to a customary practice. She says that in the Ivory Coast "[w]omen are entrepreneurs without realizing it because they sell, they maintain the family budget, they implement actions that are really entrepreneurial actions without being told that it is entrepreneurship". Others, like Ana Maria, want to see in social entrepreneurship, if not a reserved area, a space in which being a woman would be an asset: "I'm single. I fought by myself and I want to mention that the fact that I'm a woman didn't let me down. I don't think that it's a point of weakness [...] being a woman in social entrepreneurship, it can even be a strength because it's social and I think that women have an inclination to help the community."

While some see social entrepreneurship as second nature to women, others point out how difficult it is to reconcile entrepreneurship with social gender norms. Many described, not without humor, how much people prefer to send them back to domestic work and restrict them inside the house rather than allow them into the economic sphere and entrepreneurship. Pauline says, for example, that she is often asked by competition committees: "[a]re you [being] supported?" She elaborates that "most often, it's funny, it's men who ask this question! I want to tell them: and what about you, are you supported by your wife?" The apprehension of social and societal norms refers in turn to the personal and sometimes cultural history of women. All show how much the relationship to femininity and the gendered societal constraints associated with women are questioned by the entrepreneurial approach.

4.3.3. *Individual conversion factors*

The entrepreneurial path also challenges individual capacities. The women's stories nourish a variety of discourses and deal with different types of elements. For some, coming from the deprived areas is a strength. The territory, its specificities and its difficulties are an additional advantage for some women, such as Fatoumata: "An entrepreneur is a person who already dares. [...] Me personally, where I grew up in the suburbs, it is not pejorative; on the contrary, it is a great wealth, it is true that, for us, it is another world. With the experience I had, it wasn't too difficult for me to get started and create my own business." For others, this imprint of the neighborhood territory makes things more complex, and the path to entrepreneurship is akin to learning a new language:

> My difficulty, as a woman from the suburbs who didn't get to go to the best schools, is the language within the incubator. When you arrive, they tell you: no, but Yamina, with what you do, you must have a 'job-to-be-done' attitude, otherwise you cannot do your 'pricing'. Then, you look at him with a lot of distress, and you say to him: can you translate into French for me? It's very coded (Yamina).

For all of the women we interviewed, improving self-confidence was necessary for business creation. Pauline regrets somewhat engaging in self-censorship, while Ana Maria states that she had to overcome her "inferiority complex". To take action and feel free to do so, women often have to break free of their internal barriers. The development of this self-confidence is tied to the need for training, as illustrated by Naomie. While she is, at first glance, in an ideal situation for entrepreneurship (support from her spouse and children and solid professional experience that has enabled her to develop a vast network), she feels the need for training and tells of having taken intensive Massive Open Online Courses (MOOCs) in entrepreneurship over two and a half months before feeling ready to borrow from her friends and family and present her project to a bank.

In the course of their entrepreneurial project, the women noted that a certain number of skills had already been acquired. They could thus draw on their previous network or on the network of contacts they were able to build from the training. Nevertheless, this path to creation is strewn with rough edges and many of them express how the environmental, social and individual spheres constantly overlap. It is difficult to separate and distinguish these three foundational elements of a territory from one another.

4.4. The contribution of capabilities and the question of granularity

In light of our results, women's entrepreneurship in the deprived areas appears to be decisive, in its process, for the promotion of capabilities. It is therefore a positive dynamic that is put in place to help women and their projects evolve, as well as the territory.

Training is a key conversion factor and crystalizes women's capabilities for entrepreneurship. During the training sessions, women are able to perceive and become aware of the opportunities and skills they have at their disposal. As they develop entrepreneurial actions, women become the architects of their territory. The women and the environment shape each other over time. The capabilities of the inhabitants unfold and gradually redesign the territory in which they have taken shape. The infrastructure created by the association that deploys these training actions represents a decisive, but not sufficient, conversion factor – it is one of the links in a larger chain of actors who promote the emergence of entrepreneurial projects.

Our work characterizes women as unique inhabitants of the deprived areas. This research proposes an extension of sociological research, which, in the city's political districts, notes that "women want to change their living conditions and those of their environment. They are trying to bridge the gap between the culture of origin and the culture of the host country and to fight against the rise of fundamentalisms and the deterioration of social life" (Hersent and Rita-Soumbou 2011, p. 211). In the dynamics of the territory, as well as in the dynamics of inclusion, it is the inhabitants who, through their participation and their civic actions, make society. Our research shows the importance of territory in the production of action and how space, being understood subjectively, is complex (Bouchard et al. 2007). By adopting this understanding of territory conceived by the actors, the territory becomes an element of operation, a part of the equation of capabilities that can either set people free or, on the contrary, constrain them. In this way, the proposed research responds to the call for better contextualization of entrepreneurship research (Welter 2010).

Well beyond the time allocated to training, the "entrepreneuring" of the women we met represents a tool for generating an inclusive territory. Indeed, these women proposed a mode of social inclusion through action. In parallel to the process of social entrepreneurship, we simultaneously observed a "participatory" process of social inclusion (Bauer 2015). Our research supports Bauer's idea of a dual process of social inclusion, related to both the individual and the environment. The accounts we collected show how much social inclusion is a matter of growing both the individual's capacity to act and the environment's capacity to welcome. The action and its potential for evolution are thus found on two levels with two dynamics of their own that may or may not feed each other.

Our research highlights the processual dimension of the entrepreneurial approach and its effects on both the capabilities of women and the territory in question. We are witnessing a dynamic of empowerment that we characterize as "empowering". As an environmental factor, the territory, by exposing its shortcomings, its flaws and its gaps, becomes conducive to the proliferation of ideas for social entrepreneurship and to taking action. Some women go further and claim that being a suburban entrepreneur is a strength. They encourage the study of the perception of the territory as a central element and the multiplication of social experimentsm such as training, in order to make the inhabitants give to the territory new capabilities. Deprived areas are then perceived as territories with wealth and potential that are yet to be realized. The different life paths of the women show that obstacles can become advantages for taking action and that in this process the environment is not neutral.

The empowering dynamic gives a new impetus to emancipation for and through the territory. Our research questions the scale of the inclusive territory, its borders, its outlines and its porosity in a temporal approach. The micro-level approach we have taken invites us to conceive the granularity of the inclusive territory as a space where people interact and exchange in order to participate in the territory. It is the territory within which women feel it is legitimate to undertake action. Then, as the entrepreneurial project evolves, we clearly see the boundaries of this territory expanding. Entrepreneurship and inclusion often overlap and intertwine: the entrepreneurial goals push them to cross boundaries that the women had forbidden themselves from crossing, and in order to advance their project, the women reinvest in their territory, expanding it, moving around and meeting with city actors and modifying their relationship with the public space.

4.5. Conclusion

This interpretative approach to the territory leads us to consider the existence of diverse spaces that depend on how the actors choose to represent themselves and experience the space (Taylor and Spicer 2007). The comments collected and the sensitive approach reflect the reciprocal influence of women entrepreneurs and the territory. Our work illustrates the methods which women entrepreneurs use to appropriate and modify the territory of the neighborhood as a place of "contestation where emancipatory ideas are explored" (Hjorth 2005 in Notais and Tixier 2019, p. 211).

This work invites us to continue our research by insisting on the reciprocal co-construction of the territory and entrepreneurship. The apprehension of territory and, more generally, of space as a key element seems to us to be particularly rich with potential contributions to research in entrepreneurship.

4.6. References

Bauer, F. (2015). Inclusion et planification : vers un territoire inclusif. *Vie sociale*, 3, 71–80.

Bertaux, D. (1997). *Les récits de vie : perspective ethnosociologique.* Nathan, Paris.

Bouchard, M., Carriere, J., Klein, J.L., Marceau, S.G., Michaud, V., Saucier, C. (2007). L'économie sociale et le territoire. *Revue Organisations et territoires*, 16(1), 5–12.

Clément, G. and Valegeas, F. (2017). De quoi la "ville inclusive" est-elle le nom ? Exploration d'un concept émergent à partir de discours scientifiques et opérationnels. *Métropoles*, 20.

Clerc, V. and Deboulet, A. (2018). Quel nouvel agenda urbain pour les quartiers précaires ? La fabrique des accords internationaux sur l'urbanisation pour la conférence Habitat III. *Métropoles*, 2018.

Colletis, G., Gianfaldoni, P., Richez-Battesti, N. (2005). Économie sociale et solidaire, territoires et proximité. *Revue internationale de l'économie sociale*, 296, 8–25.

Di Méo, G. (2011). *Les murs invisibles. Femmes, genre et géographie sociale.* Armand Colin, Paris.

Hersent, M. and Rita-Soumbou, P. (2011). Initiatives de femmes en migration dans l'économie solidaire. In *Femmes, économie et développement*, Guérin, I., Hersent, M., Fraisse, L. (eds). Erès, Toulouse [Online]. Available at : https://www.cairn.info/femmes-economie-et-developpement--9782749212982-page-205.htm?contenu=article.

Hjorth, D. (2005). Organizational entrepreneurship with de Certeau on creating heterotopias (or spaces for play). *Journal of Management Inquiry*, 14(4), 386–398.

Lévy, J. and Lussault, M. (2003). *Espace. Dictionnaire de la géographie et de l'espace des sociétés*. Belin, Paris.

Notais, A. and Tixier, J. (2019). Créer son propre emploi : et si l'entrepreneuriat devenait un mode d'inclusion sociale ? In *GRH, RSE et emplois. Vers de nouvelles approches inclusives*, Bonneveux, E., Gavoille, F., Hulin A., Lebègue, T. (eds). Vuibert, Paris.

Pecqueur, B. (2009). De l'exténuation à la sublimation : la notion de territoire est-elle encore utile ? *Géographie, économie, société*, 11(1), 55–62.

Pillant, Y. (2014). Inclusion : jeu de mots ou nouveau paradigme pour l'action sociale ? *Ergologia*, 12, 93–126.

Puaud, D. (2019). De quoi l'inclusion est-elle le nom ? *Pensée plurielle*, 1, 25–36.

Sen, A. (1992). *Inequality Re-examined*. Clarendon Press, Oxford.

Taylor, S. and Spicer, A. (2007). Time for space: A narrative review of research on organizational space. *International Journal of Management Reviews*, 9(4), 325–346.

Vulbeau, A. (2007). L'approche sensible des quartiers sensibles. *Informations sociales*, 5, 8–13.

Welter, F. (2010). Contextualizing entrepreneurship. Conceptual challenges and ways forward. *Entrepreneurship Theory and Practice*, 35(1), 165–184.

PART 2

The Stakeholders of Inclusive Entrepreneurial Ecosystems

5

From Fighting Exclusion to Projects for Inclusion: The Evolution of Public and Private Policies

Organizations and institutions are increasingly integrating (at least in their discourses if not in their actual practices) an objective of social or economic inclusion that seems to take precedence over various forms of fighting against exclusion, in particular, social exclusion. This trend can be seen as linked to the evolution of mentalities and the hierarchy of values of multiple stakeholders and sometimes as a reflection of a trend or mimicry that can be applied across borders. The role and policies of the various private and public actors who contribute more or less directly to this evolution seem to be quite intertwined. In order to analyze this phenomenon, it is useful to first look back at the conceptual and ideological evolution that has led to this preference for inclusive policies over policies aimed at combating exclusion. It should then be possible to identify the stakeholders who play a role in the development of "inclusive" organizations or territories, with this development appearing as a result of a collective evolution, legitimized and assumed by the actors themselves.

Therefore, in this chapter, we first analyze the evolution of representations concerning social exclusion in France and their consequences in terms of approaches to combat it. In the second section, we carry out our analysis at the European scale, noting the major policies

Chapter written by Annie BARTOLI and Gilles ROUET.

aimed at fighting against exclusion and the gradual emergence of programs aimed at encouraging inclusion. In the following sections, we attempt to identify, at the organizational and institutional levels, some of the key players in current inclusion policies. In particular, the third section focuses on the current trend for "diversity and inclusion" policies in large multinational companies, while the fourth section focuses on institutions and public authorities that rely on their fundamental missions to put forward territorial inclusion projects. Our analysis will help to show that the concept of inclusion is on the way to becoming a major axis of the new corporate social responsibility (CSR) policies of large companies on an international level, while French national or local institutions are also coming to it in a more incremental and varied way, gradually abandoning the theme of the fight against exclusion. We ask whether inclusion can be exercised in a territorial logic – in the spatial, temporal and cultural sense of the term – noting that its global (international) dimension remains the most frequently displayed.

5.1. A brief history of the fight against social exclusion in France[1]

Even though the term "social exclusion" became popular in France during the 1970s in a context of political action, an overall improvement in living conditions and changing needs, René Lenoir, the French Secretary of State for Social Action, did not use this expression in his book, *Les exclus* (Lenoir 1974). Instead, he described "another France" of the socially maladjusted individuals:

> To say that a person is maladjusted, marginal or asocial is to simply state that, in the industrialized and urbanized society of the late 20th century, this person, because of a physical or mental infirmity, psychological behavior or lack of training, is unable to meet his or her needs, or requires constant care, or represents a danger to others, or is segregated either by his or her own actions or by the community (Lenoir 1974, p. 9).

The observed maladjustments or marginalizations are likely to be characterized by certain determining elements, individual or personal.

---

[1] This first section takes up and extends an analysis developed previously (Rouet 2010a).

5.1.1. *Exclusion as a sign of social maladjustment that can be overcome by employment and the economy*

The maladjustments would then be "ineluctable" within a society as complex as French society, and Lenoir wonders if, finally, "this 'other France' is reducible". However, it is important to make choices and to define policies (which can be costly) in order to "limit, if not eliminate, this maladjustment" (Lenoir 1974, pp. 7–8). In particular, Lenoir focuses on a new form of maladjustment, social maladjustment, which can be overcome through "participation in local life". The envisaged policy would therefore be proactive, and involve creating categories of different "disabilities" (social, physical and mental) and adopting appropriate measures for the prevention of social marginalization and for providing reparations.

Lenoir presented a conception that led to repercussions on social policies thereafter, breaking with the theses of Michel Foucault (Peters and Besley 2014), who, in the 1960s and 1970s, highlighted historical processes of marginalization and exclusion of the insane, the lepers and then the poor (Foucault 1972). It is not a question then of exclusion by origin because poverty is obviously contextual and socially determined. In this vein, it is not a question of "social exclusion" but of "social withdrawal" because poverty, essentially defined on economic grounds, can be fought with economic growth through a new and ambitious policy of social welfare.

This doxa of the time was to remain for several decades: by developing employment (and then training programs that can lead to employment), companies and the civil services were to be able to overcome, and then de facto prevent, social exclusion. However, incentive policies have had and still have stigmatizing effects (such as the "youth employment" scheme) and, in the end, can contribute to social exclusion more than they avoid or repair it for some of the "excluded".

5.1.2. *Citizen solidarity: combating the cultural dimension of social exclusion*

From the mid-1970s, the term "social exclusion" has become very popular, particularly in the context of social, adjustment or return-to-work policies and programs. The expression "social maladjustment", in contrast, has been used less and less frequently, and many types of social groups have been victims of social exclusion: people with mental and physical disabilities, abused children, suicidal people, the elderly, young or adult offenders, drug addicts and single mothers or "single-parent families", as they were later termed. A "specialized prevention" approach, tested in the 1960s, was set up in 1972, with teams working with and responsible for helping and supporting "at-risk" populations. In the 1980s, it became a matter of providing "support" and later "mediation" and "remediation" (Peyre and Tétard 2006). Representations and social relations with regard to the poor, or "new poor", are changing: economic resources, employment, education, housing, health, and the home environment have become both characteristics and vectors of the fight against exclusion, which is now not just a question of reducing and resolving exclusion but also preventing it.

The international movement aide à toute détresse (ATD, "aid to all in distress") Fourth World invites everyone in society to discover an interior or "fourth world" by establishing a new way of conceptualizing social exclusion. ATD Fourth World was created in 1956 by Joseph Wresinski, a French diocesan priest, following his visit to Noisy-le-Grand and the Emmaus camp created in 1954 by Abbé Pierre:

> That day, I entered into poverty [...]. I was haunted by the idea that these families would never escape poverty as long as they were not welcomed as a whole as a people [...]. I promised myself that if I stayed, I would make sure that these families would be able to climb the steps of the Vatican, the Elysée Palace, the UN. It was not so much food or clothing that all these people needed, but dignity, to no longer depend on the goodwill of others (Wresinski 1973, p. 18).

He was then appointed to the Economic and Social Council in 1979 and wrote the report "Grande pauvreté et précarité économique et sociale" in 1987. He asked the UN Commission on Human Rights to recognize extreme poverty as a violation of human rights and created the World Day to Overcome Extreme Poverty, which was recognized by the UN in 1992 as the International Day for the Eradication of Poverty and has been celebrated every year since then on October 17th (Wresinski 1986, 1992, 1994).

It is indeed a question of giving a cultural dimension to social exclusion, but above all of making people recognize a culture of social exclusion. Thus, exclusion is fundamentally tied to human rights and results in a permanent situation. In this logic, it is not enough to repair, support and help people experiencing social exclusion – it is also necessary to create new social, economic and cultural conditions. This evolution, in terms of both ideologies and representations, constitutes a very important break with previous approaches because exclusion is no longer being considered in an individual way but is understood through its collective dimension. In other words, we can no longer say that social exclusion can be alleviated or overcome through specific and personal measures because now we cannot ignore its political dimension: it is a matter of solidarity and the exercise of citizenship. This approach is particularly interesting regarding the current shift from a focus on situations of exclusion towards projects for inclusion, especially in the context of organizations, their strategies and their practices, which are more or less legitimized by their members.

5.1.3. *Market exclusion: an indicator of long-term unemployment questioning social rights*

The French National Institute of Statistics and Economic Studies (Institut national des statistiques des études économiques (INSEE)) introduced the notion of exclusion from the market (Didier 1996)[2]. Measurable and solid (even robust) variables would therefore make it possible to highlight thresholds linked to levels of exclusion, usable above all for the labor market and the identification of "exclusionary unemployment", lasting exclusion from the labor market through very long-term unemployment, observed in particular for older or unskilled workers (Freyssinet 2004). These situations can lead to a deterioration in work skills and even a loss of motivation to seek any kind of employment.

This notion of "market exclusion" can be analyzed as an instrumentalization of the notion of exclusion, which is reduced to a measurement of the "employment" (rather than "work") variable and to relativization of individual cases by means of a threshold value without taking into account the contexts or even any political or economic analysis of the individual situations. However, this notion is convenient, if not actually useful, for public authorities, who can define incentives for hiring "excluded" workers in tandem with other training or remediation schemes.

---

2 This term appeared in 1987 in the issue on unemployment in the journal *Données sociales*, published since 1978.

With the three conceptual evolutions described, the expression "social exclusion" has become established in everyday life and the social and political spheres and has moved beyond the characterization of the "poor", the disabled or the maladjusted. Indeed, the question of social rights quickly becomes essential: rights to housing, health, work, education, retirement, etc., a certain number of basic rights that can be guaranteed by the constitution or the law[3]. It is by creating and ensuring the exercise of rights that the fight against exclusion becomes part of a citizen's approach, very far from the old approach of assistance, but within the framework of a still very lively debate on the duty of solidarity and on its counterparts, on the very conditions of exercising citizenship. It is an approach that allows a paradigm shift towards inclusion; an approach that is a priori supportive and attentive.

5.1.4. Exclusion as a process of disaffiliation and vulnerability combated by social and family support

Social exclusion has thus given rise to numerous works, which have focused less on the uses of the expression and the concept within the public sphere and more on the analysis as a process, particularly in sociological research. For Robert Castel (1991), exclusion is like a process of disaffiliation. This new approach is transversal because exclusion and marginality are no longer considered to be a result of dependence or poverty but rather it envisages situations of rejection from the circuits of social exchange. It makes it possible to reverse this dynamic of exclusion and the possible irreversibility of its effects by detecting "zones of vulnerability", for example, following a divorce or any other situation (instability or precariousness of employment, school system without a diploma) that could have consequences on emotional freedom. Such a process of disaffiliation or marginalization can then affect people in these kinds of situations, especially when they are not embedded in a context of family solidarity.

5.1.5. Exclusion as a marker of marginality or even of refusal of assistance

This analysis is close to that of Serge Paugam, who defined the "process of social disqualification" as a relationship of interdependence between the

---

3 The debate on this subject, which was very lively for several years, led to the adoption in 2006 of a law allowing prefects to requisition vacant housing, which is still very difficult to achieve.

poor and excluded and the rest of the society. These poor and excluded people, thus designated, are characterized, in their diversity, by five elements: a stigmatization; a specific mode of integration; a low level of reactivity induced in part by the situation of dependence on the community; specific modes of resistance to the stigma with variable situations of adaptation to the assistance relationship; and fragile social links (Paugam 1991).

The refusal to provide social welfare leads to marginalization of the excluded and relegates them to a lower category of citizen. This in turn results in humiliation, with the consequence of a break of the social link. The poor are then disqualified and develop a feeling of social uselessness. The link between this approach and the theories of identity formation is interesting: disqualification participates in a negative identity dynamic that explains unexpected behaviors in relation to institutional assistance or even solidarity approaches. Thus, social exclusion can be analyzed as *social anomie* that participates in a culture of exclusion, with specific lifestyles and behaviors considered to deviate from social norms or even be dangerous for society.

As such, it is a trend that can justify policies of integration and assimilation. However, the choice of when these three terms are used is not a neutral one: currently, integration and assimilation are mainly oriented towards immigrants, while the marginalized or the "dropout" is supposed to be "inserted". By giving an institutional delimitation to the poor and poverty (new or old), programs and policies to combat exclusion can lead to the worsening of the situations of those they are trying to help, while de facto instilling a culture of poverty and exclusion. For Castel, however, social disaffiliation does not necessarily result in social exclusion, which is an extreme situation.

5.1.6. *A case-by-case approach to combating social exclusion and individual disintegration*

The question of exclusion should be considered in relation to the constructions of individual and collective identities in the contexts of communities, cohesion and feelings of local, regional and national (or even supranational) belonging, as well as that of the highlighting of the fragmentations of societies, or of "social fractures"[4]. It is thus a question of examining, once again, social links and their maintenance within societies, since even if exclusion can be observed, it remains difficult to circumscribe. From a more utilitarian point of view, it is difficult to accept that society should accept the loss of human resources as a consequence of exclusion.

For some authors, it is necessary to go beyond the collective analysis. Thus, for Vincent de Gaulejac, exclusion is also linked to a personal flaw, in particular, unemployment, However, this is not the only trigger of the exclusion process; it is a case of disintegration based on the individual destinies of the people concerned and therefore an individual process without the necessary social marking beforehand (de Gaulejac and Taboada Léonetti 1994). In the framework of this analysis, which reiterates the exploration of social exclusion, the symbolic dimension is central. The social link can be lost with this "disintegration", which then leads to the loss of an identity link. This "shame process" can explain how the people can develop strategies of isolation, concealment, withdrawal or core distancing, as described by Jean-François Laé, Numa Murad and Arlette Farge (Laé and Murad 1985, 1995; Laé 1996; Laé and Farge 2000).

These sociological analyses, which are often the work of clinical sociologists, allow us to reconsider the role of the excluded and challenge the often installed use of a global and globalizing delimitation of social exclusion, which does not take into account individual aspects, generalizes situations and, ultimately, leaves the citizen with no way to confront the otherness of exclusion.

5.1.7. Social exclusion: an inevitable dysfunction of modern society

Consequently, the term "social exclusion" has become widespread and, as is often the case with such semantic developments, has become unclear. Inevitably polysemous, the term has also been linked to a rich and varied vocabulary: assimilation, insertion, integration, precariousness, vulnerability, marginalization, discrimination, segregation, etc. However, taking into account a universalism in terms of human rights, it is appropriate to consider

---

4 The expression was popularized by the philosopher Marcel Gauchet, then by Emmanuel Todd in 1994. Jacques Chirac, during his 1995 presidential campaign, promised to fight against the "social divide".

that exclusion remains above all a serious dysfunction of societies. The forms of exclusion are multiple, and it is difficult to focus on simple, shared social figures such as the "poor" or the "mentally ill", or even the "school dropout". Exclusion is no longer really a state of affairs, but has become, above all, a process that can involve any citizen. In other words, no one is immune – there is no absolute protection, no such thing as zero risk and everyone can become excluded. Moreover, everyone can have excluded people in their environment.

The dominant and relatively old dimensions of exclusion (poverty in terms of resources and access to services, work and employment education and training, housing and health) are now part of a new multidimensionality, integrating other variations such as urban or suburban exclusion, digital exclusion with social networks, ethnic exclusion, etc. Since the 1970s, ideological and societal developments have had an obvious influence on policies. Let us recall, for example, the law initiated by René Lenoir in 1975, which placed the question of disability within the scope of associative care for the development of solidarity beyond the role of the State, or the establishment of social welfare (*revenu minimal d'insertion* (RMI)) in 1988 by Michel Rocard, then Prime Minister, following Joseph Wresinski's 1987 report "Great Poverty, Economic and Social Precariousness."

At the time, the fight against social exclusion was a political priority and the RMI had a long life – it ran from December 1, 1988 to May 31, 2009, and was replaced in June 2009 by the *revenu de solidarité active*, which was broader in scope (and then newly transformed with a recurring debate on solidarity and the counterparts to be expected). The RMI may be viewed as a response to the perceived threat to social cohesion in a context of persistent unemployment and the "ghettoization" of certain suburban neighborhoods, new forms of delinquency, the failure of the institutional prevention project developed in the 1970s and changes in family structures (in 2007, the majority of RMI recipients were single-parent families).

The expression "social fracture" was central to Jacques Chirac's 1995 presidential campaign (Emmanuelli 2002). At the launch of his campaign on February 17, 1995, Chirac declared: "France had long been considered a model of social mobility. Of course, not everything was perfect. But it was experiencing a progressive movement in the right direction. But economic security and the certainty of tomorrow are now privileges. French youth are expressing the disarray. A social divide is growing, and the whole nation is bearing the burden. The "France machine" no longer works. It no longer works for all French people"[5]. In this speech, as in other statements from this period, the aim is to highlight young people and their vulnerability – a new theme – and the multidimensional nature of the dynamics of exclusion without denying the individual characteristics at play. The social divide is dangerous, perhaps like poverty in the past; the risks of unrest in the suburbs are considered significant. After his election, Chirac elaborated on this during a speech in Valenciennes, saying that "these difficulties, these ordeals, this social fracture which threatens to widen into an urban, ethnic and sometimes even religious fracture, are not fatalities"[6]. Social exclusion therefore passes largely through individual and personal destinies, the dramatic nature of which must obviously be taken into account, and the 2000s witnessed an important change: that of the passage from the social to the societal. French policy has thus invested the field of exclusion in its individual, social and societal dimensions, linking it to poverty in all its aspects (Fusco 2007), unemployment and its supposed determinants.

The paradigm that often induces or underlies these approaches is a form of value judgment, since it leads to considering citizens in two compartmentalized categories. On the one hand, there are those who are supposed to be "privileged", sometimes without knowing or accepting it, who fear for their future (and that of their children) and for their social autonomy and who may feel guilty about their own situation and settle into a lasting fear or even a certain mistrust. The other category includes those who live in the uncertainty of daily life, in dependencies of all kinds, in more or less disguised assistance, in family or collective solidarity: some are then the new "working poor", while others settle into the shame of this otherness.

5.1.8. *From the fight against exclusion to inclusion projects: beyond a simple mirroring of reasoning*

Following this historical overview, we must note that for some years now the term "inclusion" seems to have replaced or be used to complement "exclusion". Is this a simple mirror image? In 2019, the website of the

---

5 Founding speech of the 1995 presidential campaign: https://www.vie-publique.fr/discours/220113-declaration-of-m-jacques-chirac-depute-rpr-mayor-of-paris-and-candidate (accessed: May 4, 2023).
6 Speech from October 21, 2003: https://www.vie-publique.fr/discours/141493-allocution-de-m-jacques-chirac-president-de-la-republique-sur-lactio (accessed: May 4, 2023).

Conseil national des politiques de lutte contre la pauvreté et l'exclusion sociale stated that "[i]nclusion is the action of including something in a whole as well as the result of that action"[7]. The site also states that "the notion of social inclusion was used by the German sociologist Niklas Luhmann (1927–1998) to characterize the relationships between individuals and social systems", thus noting that Luhmann (2006) reserved the term "inclusion" for relationships with systems. More specifically, this can be interpreted as "[s]ocial inclusion is the opposite of social exclusion, since it concerns the economic, social, cultural and political sectors of society".

Is inclusion a positive and advanced form of national policies, which could extend and modernize the traditional approaches of fighting against exclusion? Beyond the French institutions, other complementary and different approaches can be identified to complete our analysis.

5.2. European policies: from anti-exclusion to pro-inclusion incentives

In the 2000s, the European Union (EU) also took up the issue of social exclusion, the plural thus validating the evolution of uses as well as of concepts, representations and policies (Rouet 2010b).

5.2.1. *Community policies to combat social exclusion*

The policies for combating social exclusion within the EU Member States can be summarized with three logics: (1) the logic of functions – certain policies aim to act on income (increase in the minimum wage), employment (incentive for continuing training or hiring), education (implementation of specific support in the event of failure or dropping out), health (implementation of universal coverage) and pensions (implementation of a minimum old-age allowance); (2) the logic of the target populations – this involves, for example, taking into account the "poor" from the point of view of economic resources (implementation of the RMI), the elderly and access to services (reimbursement of family aid), single-parent families (implementation of specific allowances) and young people (reduction of employer's contributions in the event of hiring under 26); and (3) the global logics, which are more recent – the policies here try to avoid temporal,

---

7 See: https://www.cnle.gouv.fr/inclusion-social.html (accessed: March 25, 2023).

spatial or social ruptures, for example, urban planning policies, renovation of districts, installation of sports facilities, universities.

The term "social exclusion" was used in 1989 at the community level by the European Commission (EC), which linked social exclusion to the insufficient realization of social rights. This resulted in the creation of the EC Observatory on National Policies to Combat Social Exclusion in 1990. In fact, the changing use of this term in the context of EU social policy is concomitant with the declining economic situation in the 1990s, as well as the pressure placed on the welfare state, obviously linked to the problems of budget frameworks (persistent poverty in several EU Member States, long-term unemployment, changes in family structures, aging populations, etc.).

The term "social inclusion" was later popularized in this context, particularly in the context of exchanges of "good practices", especially with regard to the social and education policies of certain countries, which were disseminated throughout the EU. The EC, in its fourth framework program, characterized social exclusion as a disintegration and fragmentation of social relations and, therefore, a loss of social cohesion. Social exclusion is indeed, for specific groups of people, a progressive process of marginalization, of social, political and cultural disadvantages and economic deprivation. It is not an infringement of the principle of equality of results, but an infringement of the freedom to enjoy our rights as a citizen, and consequently, to be able to exercise our citizenship.

Since the end of the 1990s, the study of EU texts relating to these issues has made it possible to highlight the common characteristics of social exclusion and thus to be able to conceptually delimit this notion, which is part of an important ideological evolution, and which has consequences for practices in many Member States, including France.

5.2.2. *Towards an EU-wide approach to inclusion*

Where does inclusion fit in the approaches of EU institutions? First, there is a clear opposition between social exclusion and social integration because every citizen must be "included" and therefore be part of society, in law as well as in terms of representation. Inclusion is therefore considered essential, but not in relation to social exclusion, which can be economic, social, cultural or political, and which has consequences for the logic of power and identity, particularly in the labor market. Poverty, deprivation or difficulties in accessing services or goods, as well as the precariousness of social rights, are all drivers of social exclusion and which, at the community level, represent a process rather than a state. Moreover, the analysis of the determinants of exclusion is generally not appropriate, unlike the analysis of the mechanisms and institutions in charge of social policies.

The European Commission defines social inclusion as

> a process that ensures citizens have the opportunities and resources to participate fully in economic, social and cultural life, and to enjoy a standard of living and well-being that is considered normal in the society in which they live. It encompasses, but is not restricted to, social integration or better access to the labour market, and also includes equal access to facilities, services and benefits (Eurofound 2023).

The evolution is therefore radical. Social integration and, above all, the economic and social inclusion project are not really, in the end, means of fighting against social exclusion (even though they are aimed at people most at risk of experiencing social exclusion), given their great divergence in basis. Rather, they are part of a collective project, a relationship with the world and with others, with identity constructions and with the recognition of otherness.

In fact, the fight against social exclusion, under the cover of an apparent universalism, tries to achieve equality, integration and affirmation of citizenship rights, sometimes with as many hegemonic mechanisms that deny differences. In contrast, social inclusion is rooted in representations of openness to diversity and perhaps in the implementation of attitudes and practices. This collective, political, legitimized commitment should be able to preserve (or even build) a respect for particularities and differences, a recognition of multiple otherness, which can then be the foundation of a social, societal model. It could therefore no longer be a question of combating social and economic exclusion, at least on the scale of a territory, insofar as inclusion is part of the context of a renewal of the traditional capitalism and the public functions of yesteryear, within the framework of an ideal and the realization of a "social market" economy.

While these market mechanisms now concern the public services themselves in many EU Member States (which services, in the end, should be public or not, or universal?), acceptance and the claim of collective responsibility are part of this evolution. This situation would rather encourage the disinvestment of this subject in government policies, not only in relation to the polymorphism of social exclusion but also from this observation of the evolution of mentalities which impacts strategies and organizations. The political model of the fight against social exclusion, dominant for several decades, therefore seems less and less compatible with the current evolutions of society and with the break with regard to a classic conception which defines poverty and social exclusion as individual problems. Moreover, European policies now use the expression "active inclusion" more, which goes beyond and differs from policies for combating exclusion and which the European Commission's website defines as follows: "Active inclusion means enabling every citizen, notably the most disadvantaged, to fully participate in society, including having a job."[8] Active inclusion aims to address different issues: poverty, social exclusion, work poverty, the segmentation of labor markets, long-term unemployment and gender inequalities.

Finally, both national policies and actors and European institutions seem to want to implement inclusion approaches that are not simply based on the fight against exclusion by means of integrating projects but which recognize and value the diversity of situations and issues of specific individuals or groups of actors.

5.3. Corporate dynamics and inclusive policies

Society would therefore be represented (if not always experienced as such) as having to be inclusive and, above all, inclusion would no longer be the role of specialists or dedicated services, more or less legitimized, but indeed the business of all. It seems to increasingly be the case that, beyond national or international public institutions and administrations, companies and organizations have taken up the theme of inclusion themselves. In the vein of Perroux's work (1973), we can view public or private organizations as "active units" that are capable, through their action, of modifying their environment and the behavior of other organizations with which they are in contact. Yet, today, there seems to be a significant trend in which companies are playing a major role in the deployment of inclusion policies within their own environment and even perhaps more widely through a certain phenomenon of diffusion or mimicry, in the sense of the neo-institutional

---

8 See: https://ec.europa.eu/social/main.jsp?catId=1059&langId=fr (accessed: March 25, 2023).

approach promoted in particular by DiMaggio and Powell (1983). In fact, we will see in the following that today most large multinational corporations make statements with a strategic vocation on their inclusion policies, thus creating a certain movement of standardization, more or less linked to CSR approaches.

5.3.1. *Inclusion as a CSR variable*

The strategies, discourses and practices of companies can, as has been the case for several decades, be part of public policies to fight against exclusion (to promote employment in certain territories, for example) by helping promote various mechanisms (such as tax exemption, lower social charges, etc.) initiated by local authorities and the State. The strengthening of an awareness of collective and individual responsibilities, in relation to others, society and nature, is concomitant with this observed shift from a fight against exclusion to processes and mechanisms of inclusion. In a society where the forms of employment are changing (multi-activity, digital platforms, etc.), it is a question of establishing a new link between employment, work and activity, in particular through employability, a factor of inclusion.

The development of these approaches (and the generalization of a new hierarchy of values), often summarized by the term CSR, leads to different ways of functioning within different types of organizations (Hermel and Bartoli 2013). In addition to public inclusion policies, it is the companies themselves that act according to their own approaches, without necessarily uniting their actions but in specific dynamics that can be influenced by territorial, competitive, partnership or network logics. Inclusion in the territories is then determined by the strategies and practices of the organizations concerned, and public policies can no longer make use of the same incentives (e.g. for hiring).

In this context, companies are trying, first of all, to align their actions and strategies with the public display of their "social responsibility" and the resulting image issue. The question is no longer to encourage effectively but to seek a certain compatibility. The inclusive company seems to be convinced of the importance (even the obligation) of implementing a policy of non-discrimination, respect for diversity and solidarity with different social groups or groupings. This is a question of inclusion in the sense that the organization is likely to reinforce or put in place a situation of acceptance of all differences, knowing that it is a question here of the employability of the workforce. The pendulum has therefore swung once again: from measures to combat exclusion to employability and, consequently, inclusion. Thus, companies also seem to seize the objective of inclusion, and they sometimes integrate it into their CSR policies or make it a specific managerial topic.

5.3.2. *"Diversity and inclusion": the new managerial policies of large multinational companies*

The case of multinational companies is quite significant from this point of view. Indeed, a certain "ground swell" can be identified in the new managerial policies of these companies, many of which now display in their general policy a double objective of diversity and inclusion. Is this a passing trend or a necessary evolution of topicality? The question may arise because speeches today frequently include the expression "diversity and inclusion" (sometimes even summed up as "D&I") as an imperative from which multinationals cannot escape.

Table 5.1 presents 30 examples found in 2019 on the websites of large multinational companies, all of which had a specific page dedicated to D&I. First of all, we note the similarity of the discourses displayed, which contrasts with the heterogeneity of the sectors of activity, sizes and origins of the companies concerned. For example, the website of L'Oréal, a multinational cosmetics/perfumery company of French origin, states that "[i]t is essential that our teams reflect this diversity and that they promote inclusion. To achieve this goal, we create work environments where everyone, regardless of their ethnic and social background, religion, gender age or disability, feels valued." As for Ikea, a Swedish-born multinational retail company: "We aim to create a diverse and inclusive work environment where employees feel valued for their individuality, recognized for their talents, and can be themselves."

Companies	Fields of Activity	Title of the Web Page	Extracts from the Web Page
Danone	Agri-food	"Diversity and inclusion"	"It's about recognizing the uniqueness of each employee and promoting the added value created at Danone by the cooperation of different profiles with a 'My uniqueness is my talent' image."
L'Oréal	Cosmetics	"Diversity and inclusion"	"In order for our products to meet the desires and needs of beauty in their infinite diversity, it is essential that our teams reflect this diversity and promote inclusion. To achieve this goal, we encourage work environments where everyone, regardless of ethnicity, social background, religion, gender, age or disability, feels valued."
Schneider Electric	Electrical distribution	"Diversity and inclusion"	"It is because we believe we learn more from our differences that we want to make our ability to work together a real strength."
Axa	Protection/insurance	"Diversity and inclusion"	"Axa is committed to promoting diversity and inclusion (D&I) by creating a work environment in which all employees are treated with respect and dignity and individual differences are valued."
Sanofi	Pharmaceutical industry	"Diversity and inclusion"	"Sanofi is committed to creating an inclusive work environment that allows all employees to express their full potential. Diversity is part of our corporate social responsibility and helps build relationships between people, business and society to ensure equal opportunities in the workplace."
Sodexo	Contract catering	"Diversity and inclusion"	"These strong commitments in favor of diversity and inclusion within the company thus become levers of competitiveness and economic performance allowing Sodexo to be more innovative and closer to its consumers. Sodexo is committed as a priority to 5 main areas of equal opportunity and diversity, namely the integration of people with disabilities, gender diversity, intergenerational integration, cultural and social diversity, sexual orientation and gender identity."

Companies	Fields of activity	Title of the Web Page	Extracts from the Web Page
Henkel	Cleaning products	"Diversity and inclusion"	"At Henkel, we promote a Diversity & Inclusion approach. The diversity of our employees, their backgrounds, experiences, talents, knowledge and creativity, makes the difference, and that is the strength of our competitive advantage."
Nestlé	Agri-food	"Diversity and inclusion"	"Diversity involves obvious factors, such as age, gender, sexual identity, ethnicity and physical appearance. It also includes less visible factors, such as way of thinking, religion, nationality, sexual orientation and beliefs. Inclusion is about building on these differences by valuing and involving everyone, contributing to a common goal."
BNP Paribas	Bank/insurance	"Diversity and inclusion"	"In addition to regulatory and legal requirements, BNP Paribas has for many years been developing a committed and responsible D&I (Diversity & Inclusion) policy in all the countries in which the Group operates."
Ikea	Retail/furniture	"Diversity and inclusion"	"We aim to create a work environment that fosters diversity and inclusion, where employees feel valued for their individuality, recognized for their talents, and where they can be themselves."
Accor	Hospitality	"Diversity and inclusion"	"Welcoming others, recognizing them, learning from their differences and valuing them: this is one of the founding principles of our management ethic, which is both rooted in our DNA and key to our collective success."
Esso	Oil industry	"Diversity and inclusion"	"Diversity is a source of wealth and a performance lever for our company, each employee has the opportunity to excel according to his or her performance. The diversity of our employees and the variety of their ideas and cultures give us a competitive advantage."
Samsung	Electronics	"Diversity and inclusion"	"We are creating the future by fostering a diverse culture that drives our sustainable growth."

From Fighting Exclusion to Projects for Inclusion 93

Companies	Fields of Activity	Title of the Web Page	Extracts from the Web Page
Alstom	Railway industry	"Diversity and inclusion"	"Alstom is an international company. Wherever the group operates, in all our businesses and product lines, we aim to create an inclusive culture in which diversity is recognized and valued."
Apple	Electronics	"Inclusion and diversity"	"Humanity is plural not singular. The best way the world works is everybody in. Nobody out."
Accenture	Consulting	"Inclusion and diversity: equality drives innovation"	"Inclusion and diversity are fundamental to our culture and core values. Our rich diversity makes us more innovative and more creative, which helps us better serve our clients and our communities. We believe that no one should be discriminated against because of their differences, such as age, ability, ethnicity, gender, gender identity and expression, religion or sexual orientation."
Airbus	Aeronautics	"Inclusion and diversity"	"Inclusion is a working environment where all employees are respected and valued for their distinctive characteristics and have a sense of belonging in their team and in their company. At Airbus, diversity is a core part of our identity. More than 130 nationalities are represented, and more than 20 languages are spoken within the company. Our employee resource group [...] manages such topics as work-life balance, career development, integration of disabled employees, furthering gender balance and ensuring company commitment to our LGBTI charter."
Johnson & Johnson	Pharmacy/paramedical	"Inclusion and diversity"	"Diversity at Johnson & Johnson is about your unique perspective. It's about you, your colleagues and the world we care for – all backgrounds, beliefs and the entire range of human experience – coming together. Inclusion at Johnson & Johnson is about creating a deep sense of belonging."

Companies	Fields of Activity	Title of the Web Page	Extracts from the Web Page
Estée Lauder	Cosmetics	"Inclusion and diversity"	"We recognize that inclusion and diversity are natural extensions of our company values and must be fully embedded in our culture and our business strategy. With consumers in 150 countries and territories, it is essential that we continue to have a diverse workforce that understands local relevance and the changing beauty needs of all our global consumers."
Amazon	Electronic commerce	"Diversity and inclusion"	"Amazon has always been and always will be committed to diversity and inclusion. We seek builders from all backgrounds to join our teams and we encourage our employees to bring their authentic, original and best selves to work."
Mercedes-Benz	Automotive industry	"Diversity and inclusion"	"We strive to create an open atmosphere that welcomes diverse points of view and promotes dialogue. This encourages the kind of innovative thinking that enables us to best serve our customers, dealers and each other every day. Cultivating a culture of inclusion is a core commitment for Mercedes-Benz Financial Services, and it is a business imperative."
H&M	Clothing	"Diversity and inclusion"	"Inclusion is diversity in action. To us, that is why inclusion comes first. Diversity is the mix of people while inclusion is about making that mix work. In an inclusive and diverse environment, we can all contribute to optimizing our decision-making and team performance by reflecting, respecting and relating to our employees, customers and communities."
HSBC	Finance/insurance	"Diversity and inclusion"	"Diversity is in our roots. HSBC was founded more than 150 years ago to finance trade between Europe and Asia, and we continue to bring different people and cultures together."
Maersk	Transportation/energy	"Diversity and inclusion"	"We aspire to create an inclusive culture where employees from every background can contribute to their fullest. In doing this, we will be in a prime position to attract people from the widest talent pool, specifically increasing the gender and nationality diversity at our senior levels."

From Fighting Exclusion to Projects for Inclusion   95

Companies	Fields of Activity	Title of the Web Page	Extracts from the Web Page
Nike	Sports equipment	"Diversity and inclusion"	"At Nike, we believe that diversity fosters creativity and accelerates innovation. We value the unique backgrounds and experiences everyone brings, and want all who join us to realize their full potential. Because different perspectives can fuel the best ideas, we are committed to a workplace that is increasingly diverse and inclusive."
Microsoft	Computer science	"Diversity and inclusion"	"We believe in the transformative power of diversity and inclusion. Only by actively engaging different perspectives can we challenge and stretch our thinking, enrich the experiences of our employees, and empower every person and every organization on the planet to achieve more."
Thyssenkrupp	Steel industry	"Diversity and inclusion"	"We believe that different cultures enrich us and make working together more enjoyable and more successful. We are committed to a corporate policy that values, supports, and utilizes diversity."
Coca-Cola	Non-alcoholic beverages	"Diversity and inclusion"	"Be as inclusive and as diverse as our brands, unleashing the power of perspectives within the associates to drive innovation and sustainable system growth. Mirror the richly diverse markets we serve, capitalizing on our inclusive culture to attract, develop, engage and retain a global talent mix to fuel our competitive advantage."
General Motors	Automotive industry	"Diversity and inclusion"	"A winning culture of inclusion that naturally enables GM employees, suppliers, dealers and communities to fully contribute in the pursuit of total customer enthusiasm."
Marsh and McLennan	Insurance/risk management	"Diversity and inclusion"	"Each employee of the company has a unique personality, we respect the staff and believe that having different perspectives, opinions and practical skills will help us improve the quality of services we provide to our clients."

Table 5.1. *Extracts from the sites of 30 multinational companies*

This overview shows that despite the variety of companies in terms of sectors of activity, size or geographical origin, there is great similarity in the discourse on inclusive policies, which are presented as guarantees of respect for diversity. Thus, we can see that inclusion policies are more or less linked to the "social responsibility of companies and organizations, to what some researchers call the power of discourses on diversity at work" (Zanoni and Janssens 2015) thanks to which the multinational company of the 21st century can thereby regain a certain form of legitimacy. It can also be noted, following on from Goxe and Viegas Pires (2019), that when the demographic or social characteristics of the policy are described, they mainly concern disability, gender and nationality, which could lead to the paradox of taking into account certain special needs of social groups, which is likely to recreate some common categorical norms.

Considering the systematic association of the concept of inclusion with that of diversity in corporate discourse, it seems that the clarification provided by the multinational corporation H&M is quite unique: "Diversity is the mixing of people, while inclusion is making this mix work. The legitimacy of the association of the two principles in general policies would therefore be based on their need for operationality." More specifically, we can find here the appearance of what DiMaggio and Powell (1983) term the phenomenon of "isomorphism" – a key concept in the neo-institutional approach. Isomorphic processes lead units to resemble each other more and more under the influence of institutions, norms or mimicry. We may wonder, in the present case, about the existence of a logic of mimetic isomorphism, which would lead large companies to imitate each other and become increasingly similar vis-à-vis "diversity and inclusion" policies, although these organizations are led by leaders convinced of the merits of such orientations. If we then wonder about the application of this type of approach at the level of territorial public organizations, it is the local authorities that are also concerned. What role do they play in inclusive dynamics, and are they, like companies, subject to marked movements in this area?

5.4. Public policies for inclusion at the territorial level

The term "inclusive city" stands out as an initial approach to inclusion at the territorial level. According to Clément and Valegeas (2017), what is presented as a concept would in fact be more of a watchword for action and "a means of rationalizing the urban project". The authors draw on the work of Herman Van der Wusten (2016) who situates the "inclusive city" within a set of possible urban models. In particular, the formalization of this model came from the UN Habitat program, which has worked to develop the idea of inclusive cities since the early 2000s (UN Habitat 2001).

5.4.1. *The development of the "inclusive city"*

For Van der Wusten (2016), the "inclusive city" constitutes an alternative path, more political and citizen-oriented, which would lie between New Public Management (with its managerial approaches) and the principles of "good governance" (resulting from the mimetic influence of international institutions). We can view the model of the inclusive city as more or less corresponding to a logic of citizenship aimed at involving all inhabitants in the public sphere; the approach is more one of citizen participation in the affairs of the territory. Clément and Valegeas (2017) conclude that "the term 'inclusive' seems to come at a time when the idea of fighting exclusion is beginning to run out of steam, by presenting its positive side", with the threat of being faced with a catch-all word that would have the merit of being consensual but would run the risk of remaining empty of meaning. Nevertheless, the term "inclusive city" now seems to be widely used, both by local authorities and by companies wishing to promote their services within the lives of the citizenry.

Which city policies explicitly include the principle of inclusion in their objectives? It seems to be common in North America: in Canada, several communities have identified themselves as inclusive cities. For example, according to its 2018–2021 action plan, Montreal is primarily focused on newcomers to the city: "The integration of newcomers to Montreal is everyone's business!"[9] In the United States, research on the inclusive city (Poethig et al. 2018) highlights two criteria: economic inclusion and racial inclusion, which together make an overall inclusion index. The researchers explain their choice of these two criteria by the fact that it is common for

---

9 City of Montreal (2018). Montréal inclusive, Plan d'action 2018–2021: https://www.coe.int/ en/web/interculturalcities/-/la-ville-de-montreal-devoile-son-premier-plan-d-action-en-matiere-d-immigration-et-d-integration-des-nouveaux-arrivants (accessed: September 21, 2021).

US cities to experience economic growth while leaving out certain groups, particularly communities of color, given the long history of discrimination in the country. In this framework, economic inclusion refers to the ability of low-income residents to contribute to and benefit from economic prosperity, which is measured by income distribution, housing affordability, the proportion of poor residents and high school dropout rates.

In France, several cities or metropolises, such as Paris, Lyon, Dijon and even Bordeaux, present themselves as "inclusive cities" by demonstrating an awareness of the issues of accessing the services within the urban territory. In 2016, Anne Hidalgo, Mayor of Paris, defined the inclusive city as follows:

> In our cities, a wide variety of populations live together: cosmopolitan creative people who take advantage of globalization; fragile populations who come to the city to find refuge and resources that do not exist outside; and the middle classes, the employeess of public services as well as the private sector, who make the city function. We need to keep the equity, to ensure that everyone can live together. A city that is doing well relies on the diversity of its inhabitants[10].

Within this quote, we find the combination of inclusion and diversity. These analyses also show a certain territorial specificity of the concept of inclusive city, insofar as the concept and the criteria associated with it do not seem to be found as much in other countries or regions of the world, or perhaps not yet if the phenomenon of mimetic isomorphism mentioned above has not yet had time to take effect.

5.4.2. *Towards a societal role for local authorities*

Beyond the policy of a municipality or metropolis on its own inclusive approach, in terms of services to its inhabitants, the role of local authorities in the inclusive development of societies can also be highlighted. According to Jean-Marc Berthet (2018), it is a matter of thinking about the conditions of access to society: "But these conditions of access invite a reversal of the burden of proof: it is no longer up to individuals to deploy all their resources

---

10 See: https://www.latribune.fr/regions/ile-de-france/la-ville-inclusive-c-est-la-reponse-aux-defis-du-xxie-siecle-617902.html (accessed: March 25, 2023).

to gain access, but rather up to the city, the society and the school to create the conditions that allow for this generalized accessibility." This logic of a societal role to be played by local authorities with regard to inclusion thus seems to be developing. In 2016, Paris hosted a global summit "Cities for All", with the support of the United Nations and the OECD, which led to the drafting of an international call for political, economic and social inclusion and aimed to encourage the implementation of the principles discussed in Box 5.1[11].

Individual rights and participatory democracy

Fight against gender inequality, discrimination, social precariousness; reception and integration of refugee families; participatory democracy and "civil tech"; access to public data; etc.

Creating opportunities for all

Access to education and continuous training; creation of activity for all; social coverage; development of intergenerational relations; etc.

Improving access to essential services and urban living conditions

Access to housing and healthcare; the fight against segregation and pollution; making culture and sport available to all; etc.

Box 5.1. *Call for political, economic and social inclusion*

This call emphasized the idea that local authorities have a particular responsibility to encourage and help develop "inclusive territories". The OECD also emphasized the role played by local authorities, pointing out that while cities are generators of social and economic growth, they often have difficulty in developing truly inclusive territories on their own. This observation led the OECD to launch the initiative "Mayors as Champions for Inclusive Growth" in 2016, which aimed to capitalize on exchanges of experience and create a scale effect. Within this framework, Paris defined an "action plan for inclusive growth in cities", which aimed to "take concrete steps to combat the disparities between rich and poor in four areas: (1) education; (2) the labor market; (3) housing and the urban environment;

---

11 Commissariat général à l'égalité des territoires (CGET): https://www.cget.gouv.fr/appel-villes-inclusives-innovantes-resilientes (accessed September 21, 2021).

(4) infrastructure and public services"[12]. The approach emphasized not only the role of the city for its own sake but also its contribution to a more general societal dynamic.

These new approaches to the inclusive development of societies highlight, on the one hand, the importance of the territorial logic for the implementation of policies, and, on the other hand, the phenomenon of collective dynamics that seems to constitute a desired and desirable driver for moving from local and isolated initiatives to real finalized action programs. Territorial dynamics thus appear as carriers of interactions to be managed between public and private actors or between institutions at the "macro" level and organizations at the "micro" level (Nobile and Marin 2018). These dynamics represent new ways of understanding social inclusion projects, which now seem to have effectively supplanted traditional programs for combating exclusion.

5.5. Conclusion

Our analysis has shown that inclusion has become very present in the speeches, policies or practices of institutions, organizations and actors (both public and private) at the national, European and international levels. Indeed, over the last few years, the principle of an organization open to diversity, willing to promote an inclusive work environment and to participate in the fight against discrimination in its territories, has become widespread, often as an expression or practical extension of the societal responsibility of organizations (Bartoli et al. 2019). In contrast to the fight against exclusion, which could lead to leveling the players within a collective project aiming at the integration of all, the inclusion policies now made explicit and sometimes implemented are based on principles stating the richness of diversity and respect for difference or otherness. National and international public institutions have embraced the topic of "inclusion" in an attempt to combine approaches based on unity with respect for difference, whereas companies have treated inclusion as a way to promote their image, and local governments are seeking to modernize the bases and modalities of their public policies.

---

12 OECD (2018). Plan d'action de Paris pour une croissance inclusive dans les villes: http://www.oecd-inclusive.com/wp-content/uploads/2018/04/plan-d-action-de-paris.pdf (accessed: March 25, 2023).

5.6. References

Bartoli, A., Guerrero, J.L., Hermel, P. (eds) (2019). *Responsible Organizations in the Global Context. Current Challenges and Forward-Thinking Perspectives.* Palgrave Macmillan, London.

Berthet, J.M. (2018). Ville inclusive : mise en perspective de 2 années de veille. Report, Direction de la prospective et du dialogue public, Lyon.

Castel, R. (1991). De l'indigence à l'exclusion, la désaffiliation. Précarité du travail et vulnérabilité relationnelle. In *Face à l'exclusion. Le modèle français*, Donzelot, J. (ed.). Éditions Esprit, Paris.

Clément, G. and Valegeas, F. (2017). De quoi la "ville inclusive" est-elle le nom ? Exploration d'un concept émergent à partir de discours scientifiques et opérationnels. *Métropoles* [Online]. Available at: http://journals.openedition.org/metropoles/5469.

De Gaulejac, V. and Taboada Léonetti, I. (eds) (1994). *La lutte des places.* Desclée de Brouwer, Paris.

Didier, E. (1996). De l' "exclusion" à l'exclusion. *Politix*, 9(34), 5–27.

DiMaggio, P. and Powell, W. (1983). The iron-cage revisited: Institutional isomorphism and collective rationality in organizational field. *American Sociological Review*, 48, 147–160.

Emmanuelli, X. (2002). *La Fracture sociale.* PUF, Paris.

Eurofound (2023). Social inclusion. [Online]. Available at: https://www.eurofound.europa.eu/topic/social-inclusion.

European Commission (2003). Rapport conjoint de la Commission et du Conseil sur l'inclusion sociale [Online]. Available at: http://ec.europa.eu/employment_social/soc-prot/soc-incl/final_joint_inclusion_report_2003_fr.pdf.

Foucault, M. (1972). *Histoire de la folie à l'âge classique.* Gallimard, Paris.

Freyssinet, J. (2004). *Le chômage.* La Découverte, Paris.

Fusco, A. (2007). *La pauvreté, un concept multidimensionnel.* L'Harmattan, Paris.

Goxe, F. and Viegas Pires, M. (2019). Because it's worth it? A critical discourse analysis of diversity: The case of L'Oréal. In *Responsible Organizations in the Global Context*, Bartoli, A., Guerrero, J.L., Hermel, P. (eds). Palgrave McMillan, London.

Hermel, P. and Bartoli, A. (2013). Responsabilité sociale et développement intégré des organisations : écarts entre discours et pratiques. In *Management des évolutions technologiques, organisationnelles et stratégiques*, Hermel, P. and Corbel, P. (eds). L'Harmattan, Paris.

Laé, J.F. (1996). *L'insistance de la plainte : une histoire politique et juridique de la souffrance*. Descartes et Cie, Paris.

Laé, J.F. and Farge, A. (2000). *Fracture sociale*. Desclée de Brouwer, Paris.

Laé, J.F. and Murad, N. (1985). *L'argent des pauvres*. Le Seuil, Paris.

Laé, J.F. and Murad, N. (1995). *Les Récits du malheur*. Descartes et Cie, Paris.

Lenoir, R. (1974). *Les exclus. Un français sur dix*. Le Seuil, Paris.

Luhmann, N. (1995). *Social Systems*. Stanford University Press, Stanford.

Luhmann, N. (2006). *La confiance : un mécanisme de réduction de la complexité sociale*. Economica, Paris.

Nobile, D. and Marín, A. (2018). *Management de la dynamique territoriale*. Éditions Universitaires de Lorraine, Nancy.

Paugam, S. (1991). *La disqualification sociale. Essai sur la nouvelle pauvreté*. PUF, Paris.

Perroux, F. (1973). *Pouvoir et économie*. Bordas, Paris.

Peters, M. and Besley, T. (2014). Social exclusion/inclusion: Foucault's analytics of exclusion, the political ecology of social inclusion and the legitimation of inclusive education. *Open Review of Educational Research*, 1(1), 99–115.

Peyre, V. and Tétard, F. (2006). *Des éducateurs dans la rue : histoire de la prévention spécialisée*. La Découverte, Paris.

Poethig, E., Greene, S., Stacy, C., Srini, T., Meixell, B. (2018). Inclusive recovery in US cities. *Urban Institute* [Online]. Available at: https://apps.urban.org/features/inclusion/?topic=map.

Rouet, G. (2010a). La pauvreté et l'exclusion sociale en Europe : concepts et politiques. In *Koren(i)e Kultury*, Bálintová, H. and Pálková, J. (eds). Matej Bel University, Banská Bystrica.

Rouet, G. (ed.) (2010b). Perceptions de la pauvreté et de l'exclusion sociale au sein de l'Union européenne. *Mlada Veda*, Matej Bel University, Banská Bystrica [Online]. Available at: https://www.ff.umb.sk/app/accountPropertiesAttachment.php?kernelUserID=ID&ID=1277.

Rouet, G. (eds) (2019). *Algorithmes et décisions publiques*. CNRS, Paris.

UN Habitat (2001). Inclusive cities initiative: The way forward. Report, UN Habitat, Nairobi.

Van Der Wusten, H. (2016). La ville fonctionnelle et les modèles urbains qui lui ont succédé. *EchoGéo* [Online]. Available at: http://echogeo.revues.org [Accessed 30 June 2016].

Wresinski, J. (1973). Dans nos murs le défi du Quart Monde [Online]. Available at: https://www.joseph-wresinski.org/fr/dans-nos-murs-le-defi-du-quart/.

Wresinski, J. (1986). *Paroles pour demain*. Desclée de Brouwer, Paris.

Wresinski, J. (1992). *Écrits et paroles aux volontaires. Tome 1 : 1960-1967*. Éditions Saint-Paul – Quart-Monde, Paris.

Wresinski, J. (1994). *Écrits et paroles aux volontaires. Tome 2 : mars-mai 1967*. Éditions Saint-Paul – Quart-Monde, Paris.

Zanoni, P. and Janssens, M. (2015). The power of diversity discourses at work: On the interlocking nature of diversities and occupations. *Organization Studies*, 36(11), 1463–1483.

6

Inclusive Governance in AOC Champagne

"There is no champagne but Champagne" is the motto of this *appellation d'origine contrôlée* (AOC) wine region, whose successful historical economic model is still a source of pride. A territory of 34,300 hectares divided into 319 villages called "crus", the Champagne wine region is home to 16,000 winegrowers, 140 cooperatives and 340 Champagne Houses[1]. From the marketing of champagne alone, the region generated a turnover of EUR 5 billion in 2019 for a volume of 297.6 million bottles that were shipped the same year (Comité Champagne).

The activity of the sector is organized into two parts: "upstream", which refers to the vineyard and its transformation into wine, and "downstream", which refers to the marketing of finished champagne wines. The actors are also divided into two groups called "families": the winegrowers (i.e. the winegrowers and the cooperatives), whose activity is traditionally carried out in the vineyard, and the merchants (i.e. the Champagne Houses), whose major function is the marketing of the champagne bottles. The transformation of grapes into wine is an activity shared between winegrowers and merchants, but it is quantitatively more a trade process than the vineyard's activity (Comité Champagne). The success of the Champagne wine economic model is due to the implementation of a

---

Chapter written by Mathilde CHOMLAFEL and Jean-Paul MÉREAUX.

1 In France, *appellation d'origine contrôlée* is a label that identifies an agricultural product whose production and processing stages are carried out in a defined geographical area using recognized and traditional expertise.

partnership-type organization, in which the stakeholders recognize the interest of the complementarity of their activities and their necessary collaboration for the benefit of the political stability of the sector. This political stability is made possible through the implementation of a system for the distribution of value generated by the sector, which is redistributed in an equitable manner to the actors, taking into account the extent of their participation in the sector. It is therefore appropriate to question the conditions that turned a local sparkling wine production activity into a complex regulated system, capable of guaranteeing its participants the means of their accomplishment at the level of their individual structures. We propose to analyze this from the perspective of inclusion and its potential implementation on the highly regulated AOC Champagne regional territory.

The notion of inclusion is subject to varying definitions, as it covers different sensitivities that are evolving over time (Bauer 2015). Simultaneously a principle, a state and a process, the notion of inclusion represents a consensus to qualify the work that a society should do on itself in order to reach a state that is not conducive to the integration or insertion of the actors who participate in it but to their flourishing in awareness of their own identity and the acceptance of all (Ebersold 2009). This inclusion results in a unique form of governance over a fragmented territory, gathering together actors who share the common point of evolving in a productive system centered around the production of Champagne wines, but whose activities generate differences that are managerial and economic, as well as social and identity-related.

In this sense, the winegrowing area of Champagne has all the characteristics of an "inclusive territory" as defined by Bauer (2015), who points out that French territories are mainly structured around various plans covering a very wide range of fields. The organizational dynamics at work in the Champagne region fall within this framework of analysis, while not denying the real difficulty of implementation according to the interests of the stakeholders. However, this influences the early direction taken by the Champagne sector towards a quality strategy (Barrère 2000), which requires for its success and the maintenance of its performance over time the application of a hegemonic organizational approach, for the benefit of its field strategy. However, the Covid-19 pandemic has reinforced pre-existing underlying tensions between actors in this sector, giving them the opportunity to confront their managerial particularities with the dynamics of inclusion at work in the AOC Champagne territory. Hence, our research question is: how does the inclusive governance in AOC Champagne show its limits in the context of the Covid-19 pandemic?

Our objective is to shed light on the considerations related to the organization of the Champagne industry – and in particular the inclusive approach of its governance – in a manner that is both theoretical and practical.

6.1. The Champagne sector as a practice area for the implementation of inclusive governance

In this first section, we present the organizational system at work in the AOC Champagne regional territory by outlining the partnership-type system of governance, which is distinctively more inclusive than other models. Indeed, it is the organizational conditions of the sector that help to reinforce this "inclusiveness".

6.1.1. *A history of the relations between the actors of the champagne production chain*

While the production of wines in Champagne is an ancient practice, its development into a productive industry dates from the 19th century. It was due to the capacities of wine merchants settled in Reims and Épernay who, having noticed interest among the elites for "curious wine", judged it opportune for their business to abandon the trade of local still wines in favor of the exclusive trade of champagne. They bought the grapes and wines from local winegrowers to make bottles of champagne, which they then marketed under their own brand name.

In their strategy of product valorization on the market, the merchants introduced an early discourse aimed at improving the quality of the wine which, associated with the interest of the elites, led to the prosperity of the Houses that sold the champagne. As such, the organization of the system of champagne production was based on a segmentation of the activities of the productive chain: the winegrowers would cultivate the vine in order to produce the grapes useful to the production of the champagne, whereas the merchants would buy the grapes, produce the champagne and market it (Chappaz 1951). Sector governance was organized around the economic principle of supply and demand. In maintaining commercial relationships with merchants, the winegrower saw the opportunity to make a greater profit from their grape production than was previously possible through the production of a still wine. Often, winegrowers do not have the knowledge or the equipment necessary to make champagne themselves. On the contrary, the Champagne winegrower is confronted with the insecurity of this relationship, which is governed by a strictly economic order. Their own outlet is conditioned by the market performance of the merchants, in a context where winegrowers are looking for both product quality and lower production costs.

The desire of the merchants to preserve a productive industry of champagne creating wealth led them to define a favorable framework to develop the value carried. This value first emerges through the production of quality grapes. According to the traders, quality is a result of the grape production practices and the terroir of origin (Lanotte and Traversac 2017). Barrère (2000) credits the creation of the AOC certification in 1935 and the eligibility of Champagne for the qualification the same year for merchants being able to impose the standardization of production practices conducive to quality on all wine operators in Champagne. The AOC offers a coercive framework for those who wish to make use of it. It was believed that the passage to the appellation would allow traders to extend their quality strategy to the entire production chain for the benefit of the development of their markets. Where the discourse on the quality of champagne was previously deduced from the territorial brand "champagne" in reference to its geographic origin (Lanotte and Traversac 2017), the AOC provides a guarantee of superior quality connoted by "an approval procedure guaranteed on a legal level and permanently legitimized by a specialized network" (Vaudour 2003). Barrère (2000) summarizes the process of setting up the conditions for creating value in AOC Champagne by what he calls a "coherent combination" based on three specific and complementary strategies: the industrial strategy (i.e. the organization of the productive quality), the communication strategy (i.e. the institution of the territorial brand "champagne") and the legal strategy (i.e. the establishment and the development of an economic power).

This global strategy was able to be organized and implemented in the name of "Champagne particularism", an original concept which includes both objective characteristics (linked to the production process and to the demand of the markets preceding this production) and subjective characteristics (resulting from internal considerations of the value of the sector justifying a particular treatment). The "Champagne particularism" is at the heart of the value creation of AOC Champagne.

6.1.2. *The Champagne region as a constructed space, bearing identities*

The National Institute of Origin and Quality (*Institut national de l'origine et de la qualité* (INAO)) defines the AOC as a sign that qualifies a product whose production has been carried out according to recognized know-how in the same geographical area[2]. The geographical area is determined according to the terroir, which is based on a system of interactions between a physical environment and a biological environment, which together bring originality and distinctiveness to the product (INAO).

The AOC is therefore a concept intimately linked to territory. The use of the concept of territory is not always easy, as it possesses multiple dynamics and is subject to multiple interpretations (Di Meo 2006). However, the researchers who have attempted to characterize it agree that "territory" should be defined as a geographic space that is the object of an approach by actors who exercise political, economic and ideological powers there and represent it according to the singularities they claim (Moine 2006). The territory is therefore a space housing a complex system, offering the characteristics that it harbors a privileged place for the production and maintenance of links between actors (Pesqueux 2009). In short, a space is a territory because it houses a society, i.e. a set of individuals who interact with each other.

In the Champagne region, the territory is closely linked to the notion of a "terroir". A terroir is defined in the 2005 *Charte des Terroirs* published by the association "Terroirs et Cultures" as "a delimited geographical space, defined by a human community that builds during its history a set of distinctive cultural traits, knowledge and practices, based on a system of interactions between the natural environment and human factors". The terroir could be confused with the territory in terms of the interrelationships between actors in a defined geographical area; however, the difference lies

---

[2] See: https://www.inao.gouv.fr/eng/The-National-Institute-of-origin-and-quality-Institut-national-de-l-origine-et-de-la-qualite-INAO.

in the fact that in the terroir these interrelationships take place around a defined product. The terroir or "territory of a product" (Prevost et al. 2014) is characterized by a fourfold typology: the "material terroir" based on a physical and agronomic definition of the environment, the "space terroir" considered in its spatial organization, the "conscious terroir" which takes into account elements of memory and consciousness of identity to define the limits of the space and the "terroir-slogan" which establishes this space as a symbol of communication (Vaudour 2003).

The typical notions of the "space terroir" and "conscious terroir" are useful for understanding the process of elaborating the geographical appellation area of AOC Champagne. The first operation in delimiting a production area was jointly conducted by merchants and vineyards of the Marne region. It led to the Marne and Axonais winegrowing areas being considered suitable for supplying grapes for the production of champagne, while excluding the dawn of viticulture, which nevertheless testified to long-standing commercial relations with the merchants. This first delimitation was the result of purely economic concerns between the desire to minimize costs for the merchants and the monopoly over the grape supply for the Marne winegrowers. It is part of a logic of the "space terroir", the definition of a continuous productive territory.

However, this would have meant ignoring the dimension of identity held by the local wine industry. Beyond the claims of the winegrowers of the Auvergne for their "integration" into the Champagne appellation area, the complaints about this delimitation are numerous. The economic significance of champagne production is not so much the central argument justifying such aggressive reactions as the contempt for a Champagne winegrower identity from which certain others are now excluded (Wolikow 2013). The legal act of delimiting a Champagne appellation area is in conflict with the represented territory of the local winegrowers who historically worked to produce still wines and later champagne. This unofficial territory of Champagne refers us to the definition of a territory as a space in conflict between politics, economy, sociality and culture, a space appropriated by the actors who participate in it (Di Meo 2006). The revision of the appellation area and the final proposal for inclusion on the list of wines eligible for the AOC Champagne label, on condition of justifying a viticultural anteriority, shows the exclusiveness of the "terroir consciousness" resulting from the experience and common representations of the actors. It testifies to their desire to live together, to form a society around champagne by virtue of the identity characteristics linked to their professional practices that they recognize and the links they maintain in the territory.

Reflecting on the dynamic process that led to the legal definition of the Champagne territory has allowed us to highlight the impact of the interactions of actors on this space. The organization of the champagne production chain, which essentially obeyed only the economic interests of the merchants (its managers), came up against the desire for active participation on the part of the winegrowers. It was thus on the basis of exclusion that the demands for inclusion were founded, since the winegrowers of the Champagne region no longer wanted to be confined to a position of actor-agents (an active actor, but not very autonomous) but rather wanted to be actor-actants (an actor with the power to act and to make things happen (Di Meo 2006)).

This desire to improve status is part of the satisfaction of individual needs through the prism of recognition by third parties of winegrowers' membership in a system in which they already participate. The exclusion from the organization of the sector for which they work leads the winegrower to claim their wish to be recognized as an essential actor of this organization and no longer exist on the peripheries. They express their wish to maintain links not only with their fellow winegrowers but also, in a game of scale, with different actors with whom they share the desire for the development of the champagne production sector, with an awareness of the stakes involved in this development.

6.1.3. *Exclusion as a fertile ground for inclusion in the territory of AOC Champagne*

It is interesting to observe that the measures implemented to promote inclusion in the Champagne sector have taken place in contexts of risk for its sustainability. The winegrowers' revolts of 1911, as Champagne winegrowers protested against merchants accused of sourcing grapes at low cost outside of the Champagne AOC, were a first ground of contestation of a winegrowing society in need of recognition. Beyond the distance due to the fragmented territory in which it evolves, this society recognized the shared wine-making activity and expressed a need to find rewarding outlets for its production. It considered access to these outlets as a right by virtue of its participation in the sector. The risk these revolts posed to the economic stability of the sector led traders to change their practices. They sought to supply their Houses with grapes exclusively from Champagne winegrowers, who they recognized as having an exclusive right in their system and access to its benefits.

In the absence of an official framework to organize the relations between the two families, the application of a principle of inclusion remains complex in practice. This is still claimed by the winegrowers, while the trade would like to see the efforts of the vineyard focus more on the qualitative evolution of its wine production. In the absence of a body to regulate sector relations, power is held by the trade, which finances winegrowing activity through the training of winegrowers in increasingly qualitative production techniques and through the purchase of grapes at the harvest. Ebersold (2009) argues that one of the conditions of inclusion is the sharing of common goals. As such, the absence until now of a real dynamic of inclusion in the Champagne sector may be linked to the fact that the present actors do not share a common objective, since the purposes of their activities are different. Indeed, the purpose of the winegrowers is the financial valuation of their grapes by their sale, while the purpose of the merchants is the commercial performance of the champagne on the markets. Those who can be considered as sector leaders as a result of their economic power do not feel the need to provide winegrowers with the means for inclusive expression. Yet, the role of the leaders is, according to Ebersold (2009), essential for the implementation of an inclusive dynamic at the scale of a territory. They are responsible for creating a favorable climate of openness and taking into account the diverse needs of participants in the system.

Indirectly, however, it is the merchants that will give the vineyard the keys to its future participation in an inclusive type of partnership governance on the scale of the AOC Champagne territory. We have specified that the business implements training resources at the vineyard in order to support it in the qualitative improvement of its wine production. This took place by establishing a network of local cells, which gradually became places of expression of the winegrower's way and learning of politics and not simply places of technical learning of viticulture. This network finds its extension in the creation of the General Union of Winegrowers, a single democratic representative body of the Champagne vineyard family. The experience of belonging to a network organization allows winegrowers to develop managerial skills and thus to compete for a position of equity in the trade while maintaining their difference based on their wine identity. The fact remains that the common objectives are still undefined.

6.1.4. *Promoting inclusion to ensure the sustainability of the Champagne sector*

The Nazi occupation of France during World War II and the control exerted by the occupying power over the Champagne industry offered the industry's actors the opportunity to bring their interests together by defining a common objective in the general interest. This common objective was the preservation of the sector's interests. The general value of the sector questioned by the political context offered a ground of emergence for a common objective to the actors by preserving the chain of value of the champage sector in which they each found economic and social interests. This rapprochement was solidified by the creation of the Comité interprofessionnel des vins de champagne (CIVC), renamed the Comité Champagne, which aims to ensure the sustainability of the industry.

Instead of being simply a reaction to crisis, the creation of the interprofessional organization is part of a long-term dynamic calling into question the structural model that until then organized relations between the families. The interprofessional provides an official framework that organizes relations between families through "collective agreement", i.e. a contract that sets out the economic and legal relations that the professionals of the sector are obliged to maintain, with the aim of sharing the value produced by the sector, for its long-term stability (Deluze 2010). The interprofessional organization is positioned as an organization that guarantees the sharing of value between the actors in the sector and works for a general interest that is at first glance economic in scope but which has social repercussions.

Rather than being just a principle, inclusion has also become a means of achieving social stability at the level of the Champagne industry. It is expressed through a partnership governance implemented together by the merchants and the vineyard. Hart (1995) considers the notion of governance to be based on the idea that, in order to maximize wealth creation, it is essential to set up procedures capable of resolving conflicts not foreseen by the initial agreements between the partners. In particular, these agreements should be based on the sharing of results and the sustaining of resources in order to help continually develop the organization's activities. The performance of governance could be evaluated according to its capacity to create partnership value – a value shared among the partners through the redistribution of the rent between the stakeholders and the reduction of losses due to conflict (Charreaux and Desbrieres 1998). Inclusion would be manifested in the ability of leaders to insert themselves into a polysystemic vision of their mission, taking into account the institutional and individual dependencies necessary for the development of individuals (Ebersold 2009).

On the scale of AOC Champagne, the implementation of a partnership model of governance is based on the collective agreement that guarantees the distribution of value among the stakeholders. It is a source of individual economic and social development. This mode of governance requires the leading players (who together define the way in which their relations are organized and regulated for the benefit of the economic performance of the sector) to collaborate with each other. This principle is organized and presented in such a way that it can be understood as guaranteeing the general interest of the sector. In the manner of Bauer's planning dynamics (2015), which use the principle of inclusion as a means of ensuring equal opportunities for actors in inclusive territories, the collective agreement, a social contract between the actors in the sector, offers an optimal development ground for resources useful for the development of the Champagne sector, ensuring its sustainability over time and the equal access of actors to these resources, thus enabling each one to ensure their own development.

The social contract, however, requires the active participation of the stakeholders in the project and an ongoing understanding of the potential issues involved in living together. The benefit of living together seems to be one of the fundamental pillars of inclusion. It questions the very nature of society, which exists by virtue of the ties between the individuals of which society is composed and their adherence to a common existence project based on the characteristics they claim. However, developing an awareness of the value of living/working together is the responsibility of the leaders, who are able to implement tools that could increase the knowledge capital of the stakeholders concerning the interest of living together. Consequently, exclusion is a testimony to the failure of the leaders to create a climate of open-mindedness and to consider the diversity of each person's needs (Ebersold 2009).

Beyond a simple desire to integrate actors into the system, inclusion questions the managers' own capacity to take into account the differences of the actors. Ebersold (2009) argues that the challenge of inclusion is to privilege the instability of the actors' needs rather than the stability of the organization which is the object of inclusion. However, the form of governance among winegrowers and merchants, which has been established as a principle of general interest, seems to be at odds with this vision. The collective agreement is based on the recognition of the actors' differences (i.e. a mutual recognition between the winegrowers and the wine merchants), but on the basis that these actors are unique. It obscures the individuals behind the concept of society that they form. The collective agreement questions whether the nature of the general interest defined at the level of the sector takes into account the general interest of the groups that constitute the sector according to their characteristics, and whether the general interest of the groups corresponds to the sum of the interests of the individuals rather than an average that might be more favorable to one profile or another.

Economic crises are regularly times when tensions between the vineyards and the merchants are reawakened and can threaten the sustainability of the partnership governance system. The instability of the economic context highlights the differences in objectives between the groups, differences due to the groups' own activities and the profiles of the individual actors who are stakeholders in the system. By studying the relations between these actors in the context of the Covid-19 pandemic, we examine the reality of the application of this inclusive principle in AOC Champagne.

6.2. A literature review of professional perspectives in the context of the Covid-19 pandemic

To conduct our study, we favored documents produced by professional bodies and general and specialized press articles in which the actors expressed themselves. We also had access to internal secondary sources that were not intended for our research (Baumard et al. 2007). The professionals whose discourses we have retained are representative of the sector and have occupied a prominent place in the performance negotiation debates: the Syndicat général des vignerons (SGV), the Union des maisons de champagne (UMC) and the regional federation of the Vignerons indépendants de champagne (VIC). We selected documents according to temporal characteristics: we were interested in examining the end of the wine year 2020 in Champagne, in the period from May 2020 to August 2020.

The choice of this study period was eminently linked to two contextual factors: the Covid-19 pandemic and the annual viticultural production activity. We chose to examine the exceptional context of the pandemic as well as the regular viticultural activity, since the growing cycle does not differ from year to year. The calendar of activities takes place on a sliding year from November to October. The long pruning and tying period (November to April) is followed by the short periods of disbudding, tying up and trellising until the harvest (May to September). The continuation of the viticultural activity without any sanitary restrictions was judged essential by the public authorities after complaints from the professional viticultural organizations. The choice of the documents making up the corpus therefore responds to the desire to present the context of negotiation of the appellation yield for the 2020 harvest and to confront it with the concept of inclusion as a means of stability and development for the Champagne industry. The verbatim reports collected were organized by theme: the macroeconomic context, the microeconomic context, the organizational elements of the sector, the position of the sector and the position of the declarant.

Four events punctuated the three months over which the study extended: the break between the independent winegrowers of Champagne and the general union of winegrowers; the structural opposition between the family of winegrowers and the family of traders; the failure of the first negotiations at the appellation yield for the 2020 harvest in July 22, 2020; the agreement at the appellation yield for the 2020 harvest in August 18, 2020.

The results of the qualitative study are presented in Table 6.1.

We analyzed the points of convergence of the discourses: (1) in group 1, the theme was evoked by each of the actors at least once; (2) in group 2, the theme was evoked by two actors at least once; (3) in group 3, the theme was evoked several times by only one actor; and (4) in group 4, the theme was evoked once by only one actor (Table 6.2).

SGV	UMC	VIC
	Macroeconomic Context	
"The economic forecast is not good, but not as dire as it was during lockdown"	"We must stress this loss in revenue of between 1.3 and 1.8 billion euros. We will see by the end of the year depending on the evolution of the pandemic"	Lack of sales due to lockdown
"It's a health crisis coming on top of an economic crisis that may allow it to reinvent itself. In three months, we've taken on six years of economic complications"	–	–
Role of the pandemic economic crisis	Role of the pandemic Loss of sales	Role of the pandemic Drop in sales
	Microeconomic Context	
"European Union: tensions are not new in the last three months between the SGV and VIC"	"In a crisis, there is always a bit of fear that contracts won't be renewed because of overstocking"	"For many years, we have also been alerting union bodies to the growing imbalance between handling and trading"

SGV	UMC	VIC
"We've been telling the vineyard for 15 years that we have to keep selling bottles because a sector that no longer has any say on the final outlet becomes an integrated sector"	–	"Champagne is the only wine region that still does not have any representation for independent winegrowers within the regional authorities."
"If yields fall short of sales, there will be severe consequences, with the disappearance of operations and economic layoffs"	–	–
Internal tensions Internal imbalances	Economic crisis Value management	Internal imbalances Internal tensions
Organization Elements of the Sector		
"Champagne has always been interdependent. Tomorrow, there will still be buyers and sellers of grapes. I've said it before, but the answer on yield has to be the industry's answer"	"The first point is protecting the value and the economic fabric"	–
"Everything that has been done for years for the industry makes what Champagne is today. It's not a matter of questioning everything, but of keeping a cool head"	–	–
Interdependence of actors Inclusive governance	Value management (the main volume)	–

SGV	UMC	VIC
	Position of the Declarant	
"The merchants are proposing low yield levels that are not in line with their own 2020 shipment projections. This proves that the merchants' main objective is to lighten their inventory"	"This loss must be shared between the wine business and the marketing business"	"My goal is to be able to state and defend our views on the 2020 crop yields because our views clearly diverge from those of the union"
"SGV Champagne, for its part, advocates for a yield level that corresponds to the actual sales of bottles of champagne in 2020 and that helps ensure the sustainability of the largest number of farms"	"If we lose 30% of our turnover, we have to lower the yield by 30% to have a shared effort. And it's not, as I hear, the vineyard that bears everything if we drop 30%. We're just asking that the vineyard take its share of the effort"	"Yves Couvreur advocates for a two-tiered appellation level: one yield for the grape market, and another yield close to 10,200 kg/ha for those who sell in bottles, whether they are harvester-handler or harvester-cooperator"
"We are asking for a yield of 8,500 kilos per hectare"	"I have to have an A volume to protect value and a B volume to protect the cash flow of the wineries [the 2021 harvest advance]"	—
Internal tensions Defense of own interests	Internal tensions Defense of own interests Loss of turnover	Internal tensions Dissociation

Table 6.1. *Study of professionals' perspectives*

	Themes evoked
Group 1	Internal tensions The role of the Covid-19 pandemic
Group 2	The economic crisis (SGV and UMC) Internal imbalances (SGV and VIC) Defense of own interests (SGV and UMC)
Group 3	The loss of turnover (UMC) Value management (UMC)
Group 4	The drop in sales (VIC) The interdependence of actors (SGV) Inclusive governance (SGV) and disassociation (VIC)

Table 6.2. *Convergence of professionals' perspectives*

We also identified the general statements made by each of the three professional groups in the study (Table 6.3).

	General Comments
SGV	Recognizing the impact of an economic crisis resulting from the Covid-19 pandemic, the SGV focuses its discourse on defending the interests of its family in a context of internal tensions in the sector and growing imbalances of power between the actors who organize the governance of the sector. It hopes that the interdependence of actors and the inclusive nature of the sector's governance will help ease the tensions at play.
UMC	The UMC's discourse has a serious tone, in which the consequences of the economic crisis resulting from the Covid-19 pandemic feature prominently. Acknowledging the internal tensions in the sector, it argues to defend its own interests, which echo as much with a collective dynamics (the necessity to preserve the value of the champagne sector) as they reveal their own economic interests (the loss in turnover of the Champagne Houses).
VIC	The VIC, while recognizing the impact of the Covid-19 pandemic crisis on their sales, uses this context to lament the growing internal imbalances in the governance of the sector. As such, they confirm the internal tensions within the vineyard itself, which is leading them to break away from the SGV, with which they were previously affiliated.

Table 6.3. *General comments from each of the three groups of professionals*

6.3. Inclusive governance in AOC Champagne

The conflict between the SGV and UMC over the setting of the appellation for the 2020 harvest seems to us to be a relevant terrain for identifying the complexity of implementing an inclusive system in AOC Champagne. Our interest lies not so much in the yield volumes submitted by the parties but rather in the underlying considerations of the demands. We observe that the volumes put forward by the parties (7,000 kg/hectare for the UMC and 8,500 kg/hectare for the SGV) correspond to the thresholds at which they envisage a discussion. These thresholds and the positive or negative direction of the discussion are set according to the needs of each player. It should be noted that the core business of the merchants, represented by the UMC, is the vinification and marketing of champagne bottles.

To this end, the threshold is theoretically intended to cover the sales of bottles of champagne for the year in order to manage stock. For the vineyard, represented by the SGV, its core business is the production of grapes, often sold by the kilo to winemaking and marketing operators. The socio-economic evolution of the Champagne industry has led to the emergence of winegrowers who are also winemakers and merchants. This threshold would allow the first group to benefit from a sufficient cash flow through the sale of their grapes to cover the annual expenses of their exploitation and the second to benefit from a sufficient volume of handling to honor their markets.

The economic mechanics of the champagne system around a single appellation yield raises questions about the reality of the inclusive dynamic, which is supposed to take into account the needs of each party. Indeed, the merchants offered the lowest threshold and plan to negotiate downwards, while the vineyards offered the highest threshold and planned to negotiate upwards. These positions reflect the existence of a variable value creation segment for the players: at 7,500 kg/ha and below for the business and at 8,500 kg/ha and above for the vineyard. The inclusive dynamic between the vineyard and trade families is built around the notion of value creation in the champagne sector and the equitable sharing of it. The context of poor sales due to the Covid-19 pandemic, which has led to a drop in the value created, is rebounding on the actors at the head of structures with incompressible operating costs. The tug of war between vineyards and wine merchants tends to be an attempt by each actor to shift the value to their side, in order to guarantee their own interests. This then poses the question as to whether inclusion around the AOC Champagne was limited by the destabilized economic context. It also questions whether the interprofessional discourse around the value of implementing a system of inclusive partnership governance through a collective agreement did not have the defect of concealing the reality of economic interests that are certainly shared in principle, but whose cursor is variable according to the identities and the stakes carried by the actors. In particular, we can observe that the Covid-19 pandemic has highlighted how the vineyard–trading partnership was challenged by the emergence of a third actor wishing to be associated with the interprofessional decision-making system. The emergence of a way of contesting on the part of the representatives of the independent winegrowers of Champagne leads us to consider that the vineyard society has seen the emergence of characteristics of differentiation among the actors who compose it, which progressively constrain the historical relations that they maintain.

The identity of the Champagne vineyard family was founded around the practice of viticulture. We have argued that economic circumstances have led certain actors in the vineyard to develop their structures and to add winemaking and commercial activities that make it possible to increase the economic autonomy of their farms by controlling their outlets to the winegrowing activity. The addition of winemaking and marketing activities induces an additional cost for the farms that practice them, which is not borne by the wine farms whose activity remains limited to viticulture. These different activities on the farms have led the winegrowers and winemakers to create new links according to the reality of their practices and the issues they face and have favored the emergence of adapted interests. The identity of the actors has evolved, and the common objectives of the family are less shared. We hypothesize that the evolution of practices on the farms is at the origin of the segmentation of identities within the vineyard family into two distinct groups depending on whether their profits are created by the sale of grapes or the sale of bottles of champagne.

In his speech, the president of the Independent Winegrowers of Champagne argued that these differences in practices, and therefore in values, are not acknowledged by the managerial body of the family, the SGV. The exclusion of the organization of the Independent Winegrowers of Champagne from the strategic discussions on the organization of the sector is interpreted by the latter as a refusal to acknowledge their right to expression. In this context, it would seem that the inclusive principle implemented on the scale of the Champagne sector has not withstood the socio-economic developments of the time and that its conditions of application have lacked flexibility; this benefits the stability of the organization, which is the object of inclusion. However, inclusion in practice depends on the ability of organizations to take into account the differences of the parties involved in its system, thereby allowing for a certain flexibility in the measures implemented to maintain the inclusive system over time. To this end, the risk carried by the claims of independent champagne winegrowers would not only be due to the expression of a group that claims to be linked to the organization of independent winegrowers, but just as potentially to the expression of third parties who practice the same activities as them without joining the organization. Taking into account the needs of the actors, however different they may be, in an inclusive and evolving system would then be the way to faciliate the sustainability of the vineyard family.

6.4. Conclusion

Tracing the evolution of the relations between the stakeholders of champagne production in the context of their construction as a society and their association with a territory highlighted the fact that the organization around champagne has experienced multiple adaptations in its governance system coinciding with periods of crisis. Inclusion in the Champagne region is not so much a principle of office but rather a means of developing the sector to ensure its continued performance and sustainability over time.

However, our study highlighted the difficulties of implementing an inclusive system over time. An inclusive system will only perform effectively if it adapts to changes in the environment in which it exists. The challenge of the inclusive system at work in AOC Champagne is all the more complex, since it guarantees the economic performance of the sector, while at the same time obliging its stakeholders to comply with its rules. Our study showed that the framework of partnership governance of the inclusive type was destabilized by the existence of inclusive territories formed on a smaller scale than that of the territory of AOC Champagne. These discontinuous territories are based on a perception of links between actors who share common characteristics and reactivate or reformulate common interests with which they identify. The performance of the inclusive system on the territory of AOC Champagne and the reduction of the risk of disputes emerging, capable of calling the system into question, would depend on the awareness of leaders of the existence of these specific common interests, with the interest of taking them and their interactivity into account. Otherwise, the inclusive system in Champagne will oscillate permanently between inclusion and exclusion at the risk of instability.

6.5. References

Barrère, C. (2000). La constitution d'un patrimoine juridique comme mode de construction d'un patrimoine économique : l'appellation d'origine Champagne. *Revue de droit rural*, 288, 601–608.

Bauer, F. (2015). Inclusion et planification : vers un territoire inclusif. *Vie sociale*, 11, 71–80.

Baumard, P., Donada, C., Ibert, J., Xuereb, J.M. (2007). La collecte de données et la gestion de leurs sources. In *Méthodes de recherche en management*, Thietard, R.A. (ed.). Dunod, Paris.

Chappaz, G. (1951). *Le vignoble et le vin de Champagne*. Institut National des Appellations d'Origine des Vins et Eaux-de-vie, Paris.

Charreaux, G. and Desbrieres, P. (1998). Gouvernance des entreprises : valeur partenariale contre-valeur actionnariale. *Finance contrôle stratégie*, 2, 57–88.

Deluze, A. (2010). Dynamique institutionnelle et performance économique : l'exemple du champagne. PhD Thesis, University of Reims, Reims.

Di Meo, G. (2006). Les territoires de l'action. *Bulletin de la Société géographique de Liège*, 7–17.

Ebersold, S. (2009). Autour du mot, inclusion. *Recherche et formation*, 61, 71–83.

Hart, O. (1995). Corporate governance: Some theory and implications. *The Economic Journal*, 105(430), 678–689.

Lanotte, H. and Traversac, J.B. (2017). Mécanismes d'incitation et de garantie de la gouvernance territoriale dans l'industrie du champagne. *Revue d'économie régionale et urbaine*, 2, 271–296.

Moine, A. (2006). Le territoire comme un système complexe : un concept opératoire pour l'aménagement et la géographie. *L'espace géographique*, 35, 115–132.

Pesqueux, Y. (2009). La notion de territoire. *Colloque Propedia, Observatoire économique des banlieues*, Paris.

Prevost, P., Moïti-Maïzi, P., Capitaine, M., Gautier-Pelissier, F., Jeanneaux, P. (2014). Le terroir, un concept pour l'action dans le développement des territoires. *Third International Science and Policy Conference on the Resilience of Social and Ecological Systems*, Montpellier.

Vaudour, E. (2003). *Les terroirs viticoles. Définitions, caractérisation et protection*. Dunod, Paris.

Wolikow, C. (2013). Pour l'Aube en Champagne ! : Les mobilisations judiciaires dans l'Aube, 1919–1927. In *La construction des territoires du champagne (1811–1911–2011)*, Wolikow, S. (ed.). Éditions Universitaires de Dijon, Dijon.

7

Promoting Inclusive Partnership Dynamics within a Territory: The Case of Territories with Zero Long-Term Unemployment

Territories with zero long-term unemployment (*Territoires zéro chômeur de longue durée* (TZCLDs)) are one of the few experiments underway in France that fall within the framework of the law of August 1, 2003, on experimentation by local authorities. Faced with the pressing need to combat unemployment, which was further reinforced by the beginning of the Covid-19 pandemic in 2020, this experiment does not claim to be a panacea nor the only answer to unemployment. However, it does have the advantage of co-constructing the fight against unemployment by bringing together all citizens around the concept of employment as a common good.

It was born not from the State but from local mobilizations. It represents an attempt to weave new collaborations between the actors of a territory and between the territories and the State, the region and the department, with the ambition of eradicating long-term unemployment by mobilizing the primary parties concerned.

Although there has been some resistance to change, there have been changes in the attitudes of local actors, which may in turn influence other territories or even national institutions and structures.

Chapter written by Jean-Christophe SARROT.

7.1. The impotence of public policies in the face of unemployment in France

At the end of 2019, before the Covid-19 pandemic, France had 5.5 million people registered with Pôle emploi in categories A, B or C (and 5.8 million in the second half of 2020), as well as between 2 and 3 million unemployed people who were not registered with Pôle emploi[1]. The creation of jobs by private companies alone is a fragile driving force that is globally incapable of meeting the demand for jobs. According to economist Michel Husson, since 1950, the private sector has only contributed to the creation of 37% of jobs in France (and thus the public sector has contributed to 63%)[2].

A very worrying phenomenon that affects various industrialized countries is also the decline in the activity rate of women and men of working age: a significant proportion of them withdraw from the labor market each year, mainly out of desperation of finding a decent job or for health reasons. The French Observatory of Inequalities (*Observatoire des inégalités*) has found that 600,000 people have withdrawn from the labor market between the 1980s and 2017 in France[3]. In the United States, the labor force participation rate fell from 65.7% in 2007 to 62.9% in 2015.

This helps to mask the seriousness of the unemployment problem:

> Most of the major Western countries are in the same boat: they differ only in the way they hide the reality of the growing exclusion of the labor market. Basically, as Patrick Artus suggests (2017), "the very important question is to know if the return to employment can be done other than with strong flexibility in the labor market and the creation of poorly protected and low-wage jobs (as in the United States, the United Kingdom, Germany), that is to say by transforming the low-skilled unemployed into poor workers". Noting that "this way to reduce the structural unemployment rate and prolong growth is not very attractive, but is there another?", the economist does not envisage

---

[1] See: https://blogs.mediapart.fr/atd-quart-monde/blog/160119/pour-en-finir-une-fois-pour-toutes-avec-le-mythe-du-manque-de-main-doeuvre (accessed 25 March, 2023).
[2] See: http://hussonet.free.fr/empubpriv.pdf (accessed 25 March, 2023).
[3] "Mal-emploi: huit millions de personnes fragilisées": www.inegalites.fr (accessed on 25 March, 2023).

any other choice than the alternative precarious employment (Goubert et al. 2019, pp. 53–57).

The policies for combating unemployment in recent decades have essentially been "trickle-down" policies (such as reductions in taxes and social security contributions for companies, reduction in VAT in certain sectors, hiring bonuses, etc.) and not more direct job creation. However, their cost amounts to several tens of billions of euros per year and they come up against difficulties which limit their results: lack of control of counterparties, windfall effects among employers who do not increase their hiring despite this aid and "destructive" job creation (i.e. a job created in one territory destroys another in the same territory or in another). The outbreak of the global Covid-19 pandemic in 2020 brought to the fore the economic, social and ecological resilience of territories, at the national level as well as those of the municipality and the community of municipalities.

7.2. Building a new common good: employment

At a time when the "commons" is back in the news, particularly through the issues of sharing natural resources and knowledge, there is a need to create a new kind of "common good" for groups of inhabitants living in a well-identified geographical location: employment. Access to employment is no longer about those who are excluded as the result of a successful obstacle course (after having overcome obstacles in the areas of mobility, education, health, housing, etc.), but rather it is a common good accessible to all who are "deserving" – even those who, despite their efforts, are facing long-term unemployment. This is why the companies created in the TZCLDs are called "employment-oriented businesses" (EOBs)[4].

When it is conceived as a common good and not as the adjustment variable of a labor market that has become more excluding than including, when it is thought out with those who are permanently deprived of it, employment acquires specific characteristics: it must be sustainable and not precarious, it must be adapted to the person as much as possible, it must make it possible to create as many jobs as needed, it must respect nature and human beings; a job created in a company for employment purposes must not destroy another job on the territory. We find these different characteristics in the specificities of

---

4 *Entreprises à but d'emploi* (EBEs).

the jobs created by the EOBs: the permanent contract; the chosen time; the financing by the "contribution to employment"; useful, decent and local employment; and the notion of non-competition of the activities of the EOB compared to those of the public and private actors.

The goal of the experimental project is to achieve total employment in each territory within five years and then to evaluate the conditions for success and the costs and benefits of eradicating long-term unemployment in different dimensions (financial, ecological, the health of the people, the improvement of the social bound, the attractiveness of the territory, etc.). Article 1 of the February 2016 law states that the effects of the experimental project should be assessed against the new wealth indicators defined by the law of April 13, 2015.

7.3. A source as close as possible to the territories

The principle of TZCLDs is to offer (but not impose) a permanent contract at minimum wage to each person who has been permanently unemployed (i.e. unemployed for more than one year) in order to implement useful and non-competitive activities for local businesses. Three quarters of the financing of wages comes from the reallocation of the direct and indirect costs of long-term unemployment, and the rest comes from the turnover generated. The direct and indirect costs of long-term unemployment have been estimated to be between EUR 16,000 and 19,000 per year for each job seeker not eligible for unemployment benefit according to the Macro-Economic Study on the Cost of Job Deprivation conducted by ATD Fourth World in 2014 and updated in June 2017. In 2017 and 2018, the State "advanced" to the zero-unemployment territories a "contribution to employment" of EUR 18,000 annually per employee hired full-time[5]. Unfortunately, in 2019, this amount was reduced to EUR 17,000.

This logic breaks with aid granted to companies without consideration. In this situation, the counterpart is direct, since the financing goes entirely to the creation of jobs, and only via companies dedicated exclusively to this

---

5 For each full-time job created in a territory with zero unemployment, public finances benefit from an immediate "return on investment" of approximately EUR 13,000 per year in social security contributions, VAT, taxes and fees, plus an amount that has yet to be determined (estimated by ATD Fourth World to be at least EUR 6,000 per year) in avoided costs in terms of school failure, poor housing, health expenses, etc.

goal. The experiment is being carried out for a minimum of 5 years in 10 territories of 5,000 to 10,000 inhabitants and will extend to several dozen others from 2022[6]. The activities implemented concern services to companies, associations and residents or are developed in support of emerging public policies regarding social ties and the ecological transition: recycling centers, waste management, local distribution channels, services to isolated people, local shops, etc. They are devised in collaboration with the employees and the other actors of the territory.

7.4. Unprecedented unanimity in the French Parliament

Remarkably, deputies and senators voted unanimously in favor of the law of February 29, 2016, "on territorial experimentation aimed at reducing long-term unemployment", which had initially been "pushed" for by four precursor territories which mobilized from 2013 to 2014. Bill no. 3109 relating to the strengthening of inclusion in employment through economic activity and the TZCLD experiment was also passed unanimously on September 16, 2020, allowing its extension to new territories. This civil society initiative has therefore integrated, through a "faultless" process, a legislative framework that will decide on, in the event of success, its sustainability throughout the national territory, or, in the event of failure, its cessation.

Given the extremely ideological nature of the topic of employment, how did the deputies and senators manage to set aside their partisan conceptions on two separate occasions and under different political majorities? Did they trust the territories while considering that all had not yet been tried against unemployment? Were they convinced to act by the actors of their constituencies involved in TZCLDs (in 2020, more than 120 rural and urban territories applied to join the experimentation)? Have they measured the importance of the mobilization and the hopes raised, in the face of the impotence of public policies and in the face of the health, social and economic crises that we are experiencing? Did some of them cast their votes knowing that, in any case, the decisive issue of this experiment – the amount of the employment contribution, which could either strangle the experimentation if it remained under EUR 20,000 euros or give it favorable conditions to continue if it exceeded this number – will not be discussed

---

6 By the law extending this experiment, passed unanimously in the Assemblée nationale on September 16, 2020.

publicly, but will be set in a more discreet way in the application decree? The significance of these votes remains to be seen.

Nevertheless, the unanimous passing of the 2016 and 2020 laws lends this experiment unprecedented strength and legitimacy, which the territorial communities can rely on to achieve unanimity within their own respective territories.

7.5. Confidence in the unemployed (an excluded population)

In keeping with ATD Fourth World's vocation to act against social exclusion with and not only "for" those who are most affected, the TZCLD approach consists of first meeting with people who are experiencing long-term unemployment to discuss (as far upstream as possible) the objectives and methods of the project. The proposal made to them is to start from their experience of work, and also of exclusion, in order to design together the EOBs that will work on useful tasks for the territory and make room for everyone. The goal of the project (and indeed its method) is the participation of everyone without exclusion. This transformation of the position of the unemployed in the territory – from being dependent on social assistance to being essential actors in the project – provokes in them and the inhabitants a change of view and of representations that is sometimes very rapid, even allowing some unemployed people to find a job before the creation of the EOB. In the TZCLDs involved in the project, people experiencing long-term unemployment have also formed associations to participate in the project and strengthen their collective dynamics.

In order to understand the unique situation of each person who is permanently unemployed – their individual differences in terms of background, experiences, resources, vulnerabilities, etc., despite the standardized image that we may have of the "long-term unemployed" – it is necessary to be relatively close to the person, especially since long-term unemployment creates a profound disruption in social bonds (the employees hired in the first 10 TZCLDs had been unemployed for an average of between four and five years). To create these relationships of cooperation and trust, it is necessary to experiment in small areas of between 5,000 and 10,000 inhabitants where people can meet and meet again, and where they share the history of the same living area and common references.

The following testimony helps us to understand how a relationship of proximity that goes beyond the usual social and institutional roles can enable everyone – the unemployed and the other actors in the project – to be on an equal footing, beyond the traditional helper-assisted relationship. An employee of La Fabrique recounts that[7]:

> I have always created my job in agriculture and fought hard with the little land I had. When I had to scale back, because of livestock diseases and other setbacks, I ran out of cash. I found myself labelled as a "disadvantaged farmer". What the social worker offers and the small loans that are very expensive are derisory compared to the cash flow needs of a small farm that does not work well. Friends helped me so that I didn't have to sell it. I changed production. These big cash flow problems lasted about three or four years. When you have to go through everything like that, it's very destabilizing. It completely drains you, when you undergo administration. You completely lose control over your own existence, you lose a lot of your ability to live physically and mentally. When you come out of it, it's an experience that opens your eyes to many situations. It allowed me to understand the journey of someone who finds themself broken down. The "territories with zero long-term unemployment" project helped me regain hope. That's why I got involved by lending land and equipment. It was good for me, it can be good for others too (Goubert et al. 2019, p. 129).

Once these relationships of trust have been established and the movement of unemployed people has been initiated, the approach consists of bringing together other actors in the area around them, not least elected officials, private and public employers, Integration through Economic Activity (IAE) actors, trade unions, solidarity associations, the public employment service and so on[8].

---

7 The EOB is located in the TZCLD Colombey-les-Belles in Meurthe-et-Moselle.
8 For example, in Pipriac/Saint-Ganton in Ille-et-Vilaine, one of the first four territories to be mobilized, about 100 working meetings with people experiencing long-term unemployment took place between 2014 and 2016 in order to raise awareness in the territory, identify activities to be created, etc., before the creation of the EOB in early 2017.

7.6. The local employment committee: a new tool for shared governance

To promote and develop a common good, it is necessary to have a form of governance that is shared between the representative actors of the territory and which is "above" the EOB. In the context of this experiment, the local governance tool was the local employment committee (*comité local de l'emploi* (CLE)). The implementing decree of July 27, 2016, on the territorial experimentation aimed at reducing long-term unemployment stipulates that the CLE must be composed of representatives of the management and employees of the EOB; the territorial authorities involved (municipality, community of municipalities, department, region); the Regional Directorate for Business, Competition, Consumption, Labor and Employment (DIRECCTE); and Pôle emploi. In particular, the decree specifies that the CLE must:

– coordinate the actions of local actors;

– establish the state of the territory's socio-economic situation;

– inform and welcome all voluntary long-term job seekers;

– determine, with Pôle emploi, the list of people concerned by the experimentation and identify their skills and professional projects;

– organize with Pôle emploi how best to support job seekers participating in the experiment and identify their training needs;

– identify activities that meet unmet needs, are adapted to the skills of the people participating in the experiment, do not compete with existing economic activities and do not replace private or public jobs already present in the territory;

– ensure the monitoring of the experiment and deliver its results.

The idea is not to transfer to the territorial level the power relations existing at the national level (with, for example, a representative of the prefect, DIRECCTE, Pôle emploi etc., who would have authority over the CLE). At the same time, actors are encouraged to imagine new alliances, collaborations and attitudes based on their detailed knowledge of the territory and in relation to the objective of eradicating long-term unemployment. This requires humility, transparency and the ability to listen to other actors and to question themselves and their institutions. It also requires those linked to national or international structures (such as Pôle emploi, DIRECCTE, local missions, trade unions, local companies attached to national or multinational companies, district social workers, etc.) to negotiate with the "traditional" expectations of their hierarchy in order to gain local power to act. For example, Pôle emploi representatives in each CLE are faced with a twofold challenge: to participate actively in the CLE, as requested by the national Pôle emploi (whereas the local Pôle emploi has not always participated or been associated with the candidature of the territory), and to reinvent their role, each in their own way, with the other members of the CLE.

As can be seen from the tasks assigned to the CLE by the July 2016 decree, it is not DIRECCTE alone that has the last word on questions of competition between the activities of the EOB and other local economic actors, but the whole of the CLE, and in particular the companies that sit on the CLE and know the local territory well. It is not Pôle emploi alone that plays the role of receiving and orienting the unemployed, but the whole of the CLE, whose concern is to offer people a collective project dynamic rather than the usual (rather individual) logic of the path to employment. In its 2020 report "Dynamiques collectives de transitions dans les territoires", the social and solidarity economy lab observed that:

> In Prémery [one of the first 10 experimental territories], the territorial management of Pôle emploi was interested in the experiment from the outset, and expressed regret that the dynamics were restricted to a limited territory, as imposed by law, which did not correspond to its own scope of action and which restricted the identification of people eligible for the EOB. Yves Hutin, territorial director for Nièvre-Yonne, sees the TZCLD project in Prémery as an opportunity for Pôle emploi to experiment with new ways of doing things: for example, by focusing on the skills and interests of job seekers rather than on job descriptions to make them a job offer. [...] In Villeurbanne, the "territories with zero long-term unemployment" experiment led the local employment center to test a new, more cross-functional territorial approach, appointing an advisor in this neighborhood who is responsible for relations with both job-seeking residents and companies looking for employees, rather than having one advisor for job seekers and another for companies.

7.7. The role of the actors' representations

Members of the CLEs have a variety of perspectives on the labor market and unemployment and often have different motivations for getting involved in the TZCLD experiment. For some, offering a job to everyone means being able to put pressure on people who they perceive as not wanting to work. For others – i.e. those actually experiencing long-term unemployment – it means breaking out of their social isolation and allowing everyone to gain recognition and usefulness through employment. For some, it means building a future for successful social and ecological transitions in the territory. For others still, it means helping to reduce public expenditure linked to unemployment and the hope of one day needing to pay less tax, etc. The challenge of the TZCLD experiment is getting all of these actors to work together, with their different motivations and representations, in line with the objective of eradicating long-term unemployment by involving the people who are most affected.

It is this collective effort that can change representations, as well as the fact that the policies, systems and practices implemented until now have proven relatively ineffective. In order to deal with the unknown that is long-term unemployment, which sets everyone up for failure, it is therefore necessary to recognize a certain initial powerlessness and to agree to enter into a process of inventing new approaches together, with the a priori confidence that each actor in the territory can contribute to the project and benefit from it:

> The project is subject to multiple and sometimes concurrent interpretations, its hermeneutic logic (understanding and interpretation of the law in particular) requiring a continuous process of learning, trial and error, temporary productions of practices and knowledge (Fretel and Jany-Catrice 2019, p. 52).

Among this group of actors are civil society and the non-profit sector, which 10 years ago were not recognized as having any expertise or legitimacy in the fight against unemployment, other than welcoming and accompanying people excluded from employment and eventually helping in "reintegrating" some of them into private or public employment. This recognition has come a long way, and the non-profit actors as well as the unemployed themselves have a place and legitimacy in relation to CLEs and EOBs, contributing to transforming the representations that the actors have of each other (business leaders of the unemployed and elected officials, the unemployed of Pôle Emploi and business leaders, business leaders of

DIRECCTE, etc.). This transformation of views and behaviors is a means and a condition for the success of the TZCLD experiment.

7.8. Compensation for territorial inequalities

Some of the TZCLD territories are urban and some are rural. Some already have a history of shared solidarity, whereas others have a history of social conflict. Some are wealthy and have skilled inhabitants; others are poor and lack qualifications. In some territories, it is the city hall or the community of municipalities that has initiated involvement in investing important resources with a view toward economic development. In other territories, it is a group of unemployed people, a group of residents or a business club who have initiated involvement with the project.

The purpose of the TZCLD experiment is to show that any territory, with all its particularities and in its own way, can eradicate long-term unemployment if it gives itself the means to do so. The law of February 2016 and its implementing decree grant the participating territories significant leeway. The challenge is also to allow them to pool their good practices and to bring them up within the national structures involved (Pôle emploi, local missions, national companies, federations of integration structures, etc.), so that they also infuse and give rise to new collaborations within or between these national structures – which also collaborate in the national animation of the experimentation of the project within the Territorial Experimentation Fund for long-term unemployment chaired by Louis Gallois.

7.9. Changing attitudes

For Anne Fretel and Florence Jany-Catrice (2019, pp. 55–56), the leeway left to zero-unemployment territories

> is sometimes perceived as a constraint in that it leads actors to act in a situation of uncertainty. But it appears, according to some actors, as part of the solution, because the incompleteness of the project leads the actors to adopt innovative behaviors "by project", at a distance from a habit of managing a "public system". With subsidiarity, a principle which consists in working at the most local level possible, as long as possible, the incompleteness of the project finally leads the actors to produce

local institutional arrangements. In other words, they do not limit themselves to taking into account rules that would be imposed on them, but they rely on the incompleteness of the rule to interpret it, create it, amend it. They gradually initiate a space instituting a localized and plural construction of collective action whose "meaning remains to be produced by collective deliberation" (Lascoumes and Le Bourhis 1998, p. 38). The actors are at a distance from a certain "opportunistic behavior" to which this incompleteness of the law could have led, remaining relatively close to the spirit of the project. It is the co-management of the project and the territorial dynamics which constantly exert a force of reminder on the "spirit of the law" and which make possible this distancing, so far, of such behavior. This co-management, which is also based on a certain "volunteering" of people deprived of employment, makes it a different object from traditional public mechanisms which take people from the angle of their administrative profile.

7.10. An unprecedented articulation between the territory and the national dimension

However, as Fretel and Jany-Catrice (2019) note,

> collective action, cooperation, territorial dynamics and membership processes do not preclude struggles, including for the acquisition of dominant positions, particularly that of symbolic authority (State/territory; region/metropolis). The representatives of the State must therefore enter into processes of compromise construction, into institutional arrangements with which they are not accustomed.

From one perspective, forms of "negotiation, persuasion and encouragement" are replacing coercion as a modality for public intervention (Enjolras 2008, p. 24). State officials, for example, see a loss of sovereignty in this process of collective action and multi-governance. In fact, the TZCLD project has transformed the way in which resources are allocated and rules constructed. The policy designed by the public authorities at the national level is transformed into a territorial policy (Autès 2005, pp. 57–70). Consequently, the TZCLD experiments are similar to a laboratory where the State and the territories are experimenting in vivo with new bonds that the official *Conseil d'analyse économique* has been calling for (Algana et al. 2020). By analyzing the local determinants of the discontent of a part of the population that is manifested, among other things, in the Gilets Jaunes movement, the CAE has highlighted the major role of the territory's situation in terms of employment in the population's feeling of malaise and has made some rather unprecedented recommendations:

> redefining the objectives of aid to territories by taking into account all the dimensions of well-being and not just economic criteria; changing method: moving away from a prescribing State to a supporting State; renewing the central State's approach to policies supporting the territories; prioritizing technical and financial support for projects initiated locally, based on local information, and driven by all the actors concerned; promoting the right to experimentation and differentiation in carrying out projects.

Agnès Thouvenot, deputy mayor of Villeurbanne in charge of the solidarity economy, employment and integration, identifies at least four forms of cooperative dynamics at work in TZCLD territories (Sarrot 2020): "Dynamics of cooperation, she believes, can be bricks of the sustainable transition towards another economic, social, ecological, cultural and citizen involvement model." First of all, it is a kind of cooperation that brings together stakeholders who are rarely brought together: institutions, companies, communities, residents, etc. This is a fragile cooperation which requires means of animation and political support in the long term, and which makes it possible to generate new forms of cooperation in other work spaces than the TZCLDs, where non-hierarchical modes of governance and those based on consensus rather than power struggles can also be productive. The second dynamic is the participation of the inhabitants. The TZCLD experiment demonstrates that it is possible to renew the forms of participation of the inhabitants in the future of the city. The third dynamic concerns economic actors – local businesses, communities, IAE, EOBs, etc. – who are encouraged to get to know each other, to collaborate with each other and with elected officials and residents. The fourth dynamic concerns public policies.

For Thouvenot, experimentation is a privileged laboratory for social cohesion and ecological transition policies. These two fields are at the heart of the TZCLD experiment, but are worked on unevenly depending on the territory. However, the modes of action and the financial principles of the experiment would allow territories to go much further towards the ecological and social transition, in connection with other specific public policies (such as those for territories with energy-positive territories, territorial projects and supply), initiatives led by the social and solidarity economy movement, eco-places, local citizen currencies, etc.

7.11. Social work transformed by access to employment for all

Another field of action seeing its practices evolve in the TZCLDs is social work. A social worker from the Thiers district working in a TZCLD testified to her increased "power to act" and the changes in her own attitudes as a professional and those of employees who had often been very suspicious of social workers:

> I have also changed my outlook. Before, I felt a great deal of powerlessness and sometimes anger in the face of the complicated situation of some people. Today, I have more of an impression that things can move forward and that they can be co-constructed with the people. I see people standing up. They're happy to see a social worker and they see us as actors in the same way as them in the "territories with zero long-term unemployment" project. I'm impressed by the speed of change in certain situations of indebtedness, expulsion processes, child placement ... People are regaining control over their situation and their power to act. We think together about what they can and cannot do. Thanks to this newfound job stability, they allow themselves to do things that they didn't allow themselves to do before, even with their own social worker. Our role as social workers is to help them to make this connection, to bring up and concretize what is important for them. We also talk a lot about health issues ... As for our social worker colleagues, we communicate regularly about the uniqueness of our interventions at Actypoles-Thiers, the results we have seen, and the change in the social worker's traditional attitudes (Goubert et al. 2019, pp. 268–269).

Will these changes in attitudes and professional practices "spread to" other social services in other territories? This is to be expected, especially with the extension of the experiment to several dozen new territories starting in 2021.

7.12. Highlighting the different aspects of poverty

The new links, practices and postures that are being invented in the TZCLDs highlight different aspects of poverty, some of which are hidden in and not taken into account by most anti-poverty policies. These dimensions include social isolation, the unrecognized skills of people, their fears and suffering, the social and institutional abuse to which they are subjected and their inability to access to basic rights and security.

These dimensions do not exist in isolation, but rather they usually interact. By starting with people who have been permanently unemployed and by gathering around them, on an equal footing, the other actors in the territory, the TZCLD approach breaks the isolation in which they are confined; it relies on the skills of people who have not been recognized or who have received little recognition until now, putting them to use in service of the territory. It takes into account their fears and suffering by collectively reflecting on working conditions; it fights social and institutional abuse by offering unconditional employment; by offering permanent employment contracts (*contrat de travail à durée indéterminée* (CDI)), it makes various rights such as income security, health, housing, etc., accessible. These territories therefore also serve as a kind of laboratory where the different dimensions of poverty and their various interactions can be observed in vivo, over time and with those primarily concerned, with the aim of eradicating long-term unemployment and social exclusion, territory by territory.

7.13. New indicators to move towards an "unknown desirable"

The commitment of the actors in this collective action is driven less by calculation and maximization of the individual interest, than by a collective or social utility that constitutes a horizon whose content is however neither stable nor consensual. The territorial dynamic that is being built has two invariants: a multi-partner and multi-level project. This multi-partnership and multi-level character give this dynamic a complex institutional form, which goes far beyond the State/market dichotomy. It forces actors to cooperate in action, to strive, through the implementation of permanent social innovations, towards a "desirable unknown" where trial and error and the emergence of initiatives reign (Fretel and Jany-Catrice 2019, p. 53).

In order to measure progress towards this desirable well-being, it seems necessary to innovate in terms of measurement tools, as advocated in the CAE's note, which refers to "all dimensions of well-being and not just economic criteria" and as the law of February 2016 provided for by advocating an evaluation against new wealth indicators. The difficulties of this multi-criteria evaluation can be gauged by reading the report published by the general inspectorate of social affairs and the general inspectorate of finances in November 2019 (Allot et al. 2019), which was only interested in the purely accounting and financial aspects of the TZCLD experiment.

7.14. Conclusion

To conclude, we will return to the work of Le Guillou and Semenowicz (2017), which allows us to grasp the extent of the inclusion enterprise implemented:

> The "territories with zero long-term unemployment" project poses above all the conditions for accepting an evolution of the social model against the current of the dominant thought. Whether it is a question of consolidating a social norm (the CDI) declared rigid, of advocating for criteria of productivity respecting the capacities of individuals, of increasing the perimeter of an employer/financier State as a last resort or even putting in place a mode of regulation in which competition would be partly managed at the territorial level, it seems to us that all these developments will require a national agreement on a choice of society in which solidarity and the fight against inequalities would take precedence over competitiveness and competition.

Through the territory and the development of local partnerships, a new model of society is being tested.

7.15. References

Algana, Y., Malgouyresb, C., Senikc, C. (2020). Territoires, bien-être et politiques publiques. *Les notes du conseil d'analyse économique*, 55, 1–12.

Allot, F., Perrot, A., Lallemand-Kirche, G. (2019). Évaluation économique de l'expérimentation territoriale visant à résorber le chômage de longue durée. Report [Online]. Available at: https://www.igas.gouv.fr/spip.php?article746.

Artus, P. (2017). Zone euro, France, Espagne, Italie : le plus urgent est de réduire le taux de chômage structurel, mais peut-on le faire sans faire apparaître des travailleurs pauvres ? *Natixis, Flash Économie*, August 25, 2017.

Autès, M. (2005). Le sens du territoire. *Recherches et prévisions*, 39.

Enjolras, B. (2008). *Gouvernance et intérêt général dans les services sociaux et de santé*. Peter Lang, Brussels.

Fretel, A. and Jany-Catrice, F. (eds) (2019). Une analyse de la mise en œuvre du programme expérimental visant à la résorption du chômage de longue durée dans le territoire urbain de la Métropole de Lille. Report [Online]. Available at: https://apes-hdf.org/_docs/Fichier/2019/4-191204015551.pdf.

Goubert, D., Le Guillou, D., Hédon, C. (2019). *Zéro chômeur. Dix territoires relèvent le défi*. Édition de l'Atelier, Paris.

Lascoumes, P. and Le Bourhis, J.P. (1998). Le bien commun comme construit territorial. Identités d'action et procédures. *Politix*, 42, 37–66.

Le Guillou, D. and Semenowicz, P. (2017). L'expérimentation "Territoires zéro chômeur de longue durée" : une opportunité pour refonder l'État social ? *Colloque "Quel modèle social pour le XXIe siècle ?"*, University of Paris-Est Marne-la-Vallée, Paris.

Sarrot, J.C. (2020). L'expérimentation "Territoires zéro chômeur de longue durée". *Études*, 4, 53–64.

8

The Contribution of Quebec's Community Credit Organizations to Social and Territorial Development

This chapter presents Quebec community credit as a tool for socio-economic development that contributes to inclusive dynamics in the various territories of the province. The practice of microcredit in Quebec, which has been developing for 20 years, has given rise to an original approach falling within the worlds of the social and solidarity economy and fitting into a logic of local development where social objectives are as important as economic goals (Tremblay et al. 2017). MicroEntreprendre, formerly known as the Quebec Community Credit Network, is the main player in microfinance in Quebec, bringing together organizations that work to support socio-economic inclusion by providing resources for the creation of microenterprises, either through local support or access to microfinance. These organizations are at the first level in the Quebec chain of solidarity financing mechanisms and are aimed at people who are economically and socially vulnerable – such as young people, women, self-employed workers, immigrants and unemployed people – and who have entrepreneurial projects but do not have access to the financial investment of banking institutions or to the standardized programs of other organizations[1].

Chapter written by Marie LANGEVIN and Annie-Claude VEILLEUX.
1 MicroEntreprendre, "La force d'un réseau dédié aux fonds de microcrédit", annual report 2017–2018, Montreal: https://microentreprendre.ca/wp-content/uploads/2022/09/Rapport_annuel_2017-2018_FINAL_WEBMTL.pdf (accessed March 27, 2023).

In this chapter, we outline the impact of the activities of these organizations on a Quebec-wide scale and discuss in detail the Mauricie region, an urbanized area in central Quebec. We highlight the contribution of community credit in this region, particularly in terms of the social and economic inclusion of clients and atypical lenders. The data from interviews with the management, practitioners and administrators of Fonds Mauricie can help us to understand the territorial development dynamics to which community credit contributes in turn.

Our research explains how Fonds Mauricie contributes to the socio-economic vitality of the community thanks to its approach of personalized support, mobilization of local resources for financing and entrepreneurial expertise, emphasizing the importance of networking and pooling of territorial resources. Our research approach is based on an understanding of social innovation as a body of practices that emerge in response to an unmet need, an aspiration or a social problem (Klein and Harrisson 2007) affecting marginalized groups in particular (Mulgan 2006).

This theoretical perspective focuses on the transformations induced by the social and political crises in the last decades of the 20th century, both in terms of the weakening of issue resolution modalities, which struggle to cope with renewed forms of precariousness and emerging social and environmental fractures, and in terms of "new practices through which social actors are providing solutions to the problems of their communities and experimenting with new ways of responding to growing needs" (Lévesques 2014; Klein et al. 2016, p. 2).

The remainder of the chapter is organized as follows. Section 8.1 presents the community credit model as it is practiced in Quebec in the social economy ecosystem, highlighting its specificities and revealing key figures facilitating the benefits of the network's activities in the province. In section 8.2, we discuss the dynamics of local development that promote the potential for inclusion of this type of initiative by focusing on the Mauricie region, giving a voice to local actors and taking an interest in data on the spinoffs from the activities of the community credit organization operating in this area, Fonds Mauricie.

8.1. Community credit in Quebec

Community credit practices emerged in Quebec in response to the successive employment crises of the 1980s and 1990s, which were characterized by a serious lack of jobs and high unemployment rates, particularly in surrounding regions and impoverished neighborhoods of large cities (Tremblay et al. 2021). The key players in socio-economic development then became aware of the intrinsic limits of solutions based strictly on the market economy in meeting the social needs generated by these structural transformations of the labor market; more broadly, this was due to the erosion of the Fordist production model and globalization. The situation was also marked by mobilizations of civil society groups in the fight against poverty. In response to these issues, policies for local development and community economic development based on partnership and complementarity between the private, public and community sectors then began to appear in Quebec (Hamel and Klein 1996; Tremblay et al. 2021). It was in this particular context "that entrepreneurship became one of the possible paths for the development of employability and that the first community credit organizations were founded there, notably in Montreal with the Community Loan Association (*Association communautaire d'emprunt* (ACEM)) in 1990" (Tremblay et al. 2021).

Subsequently, community credit spread throughout Quebec. Today, the MicroEntreprendre network has 16 member organizations in 13 regions of the province. For almost 20 years, this network has been the first level of solidarity-based financing in the province, which is known for its rich ecosystem in relation to the social and solidarity economy. MicroEntreprendre's mission is "to promote and develop the microcredit approach in Quebec as a unique tool for economic development and inclusion"[2]. The approach of member organizations is centered on the integration and social inclusion of people in vulnerable economic and social situations through entrepreneurship. Based on community and solidarity values, these organizations carry out their mission by providing technical support to entrepreneurs on the margins of traditional financial networks and by offering access to microcredit from socially responsible investments and local resources. Each organization has its own capitalization fund. The

---

2 MicroEntreprendre, annual report 2018–2019, Montreal: https://microentreprendre.ca/wp-content/uploads/2022/09/RA_2018_2019_MTL.pdf (accessed on March 27, 2023).

network and its member organizations play a dual social and economic role, not only in supporting the social inclusion of vulnerable people in the local community but also in contributing to the economic development and solidarity in territories by supporting entrepreneurship (Langevin and Jacob 2008).

What distinguishes the "Quebec-style" microcredit model in the global microfinance landscape is the importance given to personalized support for people with entrepreneurial projects. Microfinance practices, including microcredit, have evolved over time. The global approach, which is generally piloted by NGOs, offers complementary support and training services to microentrepreneurs, as well as access to microcredit and savings products. Following the implementation of the neoliberal development model in developing countries from the 1980s, this approach was gradually discarded in favor of a minimalist microfinance model that focuses exclusively on offering financial services in a profitable and unsubsidized business model (Langevin 2013).

This process of transformation of the microfinance sector has been accompanied by a wave of organizational transformations towards the commercialization of microfinance institutions and the entry of new purely commercial actors into what has gradually become a niche market for socially responsible investors and also a source of portfolio diversification for traditional investors (Langevin 2017). Furthermore, the evolving landscape of the world of microfinance has been marked in the last decade by multiple crises and major drifts, some of which have left their mark, with cases of suicides of over-indebted microentrepreneurs in Andhra Pradesh, movements of borrowers' mobilizations in Nicaragua and even a collapse of the microcredit sector in Bosnia (Guérin et al. 2015).

The entrepreneurial microcredit model in Quebec is recognized by the Quebec government, which subsidizes its operating costs. The approach that relies on proximity accompaniment and personalized support for entrepreneurs seems especially resistant to these fundamental trends that have marked microfinance practices on a global scale. The interest in better understanding the contribution of these organizations to inclusive dynamics in these territories is, in this sense, all the more necessary. Community credit practices are also distinguished by their focus on an exclusive form of lending, namely, entrepreneurial microcredit. Honorary loans, granted with interest but without personal guarantees, of CAD 20,000 or less are granted only to entrepreneurial projects deemed viable by the specialist advisors in the community credit organizations. This is in sharp contrast to consumer loans (which have gained importance in the portfolios of microcredit enterprises in different parts of the world) and microcredits for businesses (which are not necessarily monitored to ensure that the funds are used for the borrowers' business projects).

The uniqueness of the Quebec model also lies in the form of capitalization of loan portfolios. While microfinance institutions are increasingly seeking to attract international investments in various more or less specialized markets, the organizations of the MicroEntreprendre network mostly capitalize on local markets with investors in their communities. Microcredit is anchored in a vision of economic development whereby entrepreneurship supports local economies. Entrepreneurial microcredit can be distinguished as it is a form of choosing the projects to finance in terms of their seriousness and their contribution to the local community rather than the level of risk and their potential return.

Microcredit involves offering loans to individuals in order to support them in their entrepreneurial endeavors, bring a new service offer to their region and promote job creation adapted to the environment. In this way, microentrepreneurs contribute to wealth creation while also helping to develop urban, rural and remote areas.

In short, these organizations have a holistic mission of contributing to the resilience of local communities, as well as to the social and economic inclusion of the vulnerable people living there. It is here, in this mission, that the unique character of Quebec's approach can be found. This attachment of organizations to their global mission leads them to invest in generating positive transformations at three levels (Langevin and Jacob 2008): (1) at the individual level, by aiming to improve material and social living conditions and strengthen entrepreneurial capacities; (2) at the community level, as a local and territorial development actor participating in economic and social processes; and (3) at the level of society, by pursuing the overall objective of developing a more humane, united, viable, sustainable economy and a corporate citizenship culture.

These practices implemented by the 16 member organizations of the MicroEntreprendre network generate measurable benefits at the provincial level. For the year 2018–2019, 500 businesses were created and some 2,000 entrepreneurs were supported, who received 23,275 hours of dedicated mentoring[3]. The socio-economic profile of the people supported throughout Quebec is as follows: 20% were immigrants, 40% were under 35 years old, 44% lived alone, 55% were women, 49% were living below the poverty line (less than CAD 20,000 per year) and 63% had completed post-secondary education. Over the past two decades, these organizations have made a real difference in several regions of Quebec and for tens of thousands of people (Table 8.1).

Loans granted	CAD 18.9 million
Entrepreneurs supported	27,334
Jobs created and maintained	11,540
Loans granted	2,967
Reimbursement	93% (average rate)
Support and training	598,428 hours

Table 8.1. *Impact of entrepreneurial microcredit in Quebec over the past 20 years (source: MicroEntreprendre, annual report 2018–2019)*

Another way of appreciating the impacts is to focus on the linking role played by these microcredit organizations in local development ecosystems by "symbolizing the strategic and complementary resource that intervenes first in the entrepreneurial projects before the other actors of economic development, be they governmental or private and banking circles, finance the projects" (MicroEntreprendre). The presence of network members in these territories makes a real difference, since for each dollar invested by microcredit organizations in a business project, an additional CAD 7 on average are injected into the project by other socio-economic actors in the circles concerned. This "leverage effect", to use the words of the organizations themselves, demonstrates that their contribution is essential for many of these projects to materialize[4].

---

3 MicroEntreprendre, annual report 2018–2019, Montreal: https://microentreprendre.ca/wp-content/uploads/2022/09/RA_2018_2019_MTL.pdf (accessed on March 27, 2023).
4 MicroEntreprendre, "La force d'un réseau dédié aux fonds de microcrédit", annual report 2017–2018, Montreal: https://microentreprendre.ca/wp-content/uploads/2022/09/Rapport_annuel_2017-2018_FINAL_WEBMTL.pdf (accessed March 27, 2023).

8.2. Community credit and inclusive dynamics in the territories: the Mauricie region

Community credit is characterized by a very strong commitment to territorial development. Network organizations in different regions have been making sustained efforts "for their social development and economic vitality as resilient communities"[5]. In keeping with the network's values and mission, Fonds Mauricie has sought since its inception to promote the economic development of the region and the social inclusion of vulnerable people on the margins of traditional financial channels. It provides honorary loans as well as mentoring for aspiring entrepreneurs, all while maintaining an approach that is both individual and collective, according to the needs of the participating individual. The organization also maintains strong roots in its local community by providing technical and financial partnerships with various economic actors in the region.

To fully understand the role that Fonds Mauricie plays in the development dynamics of the Mauricie region, we first briefly analyze the socio-economic characteristics of the territory. We then analyze the role played by the organization and how its practices impact the region's inclusive dynamics.

8.2.1. *The socio-economic profile of the Mauricie region*

Both its history and the issues facing the Mauricie today bring it closer to the other manufacturing regions of Quebec. Mauricie was the pioneer region for the industrialization of the province. Industrialization of the region began in the 19th century and accelerated in the 1900s with the establishment of several factories for the production of pulp and paper, metallurgy, chemicals and textiles. From the 1970s to the beginning of the 21st century, however, the region experienced a kind of industrial depression. Technological changes, market shifts and international competition led to the dismantling of several parts of the industrial economy established before the 1950s. Wood and aluminum processing, the two main resources exploited in the

---

5 MicroEntreprendre, annual report 2018–2019, Montreal. Available at: https://microentreprendre.ca/wp-content/uploads/2022/09/RA_2018_2019_MTL.pdf (accessed on March 27, 2023).

region, lost more and more momentum during this period, entire sectors of the economy disappeared (in particular the chemical and textile sectors) and up to 10,000 jobs were estimated to have been lost.

In response to this industrial and economic downturn, the turn of the 21st century marked a significant shift in urbanization and support for small- and medium-sized enterprises (SMEs) in the region. The disappearance of large factories providing a lot of jobs led to the realization that the region should no longer expect major contributions from these players, but rather rely on a solid network of SMEs. From this point onwards, State intervention has focused on the creation and consolidation of a network of SMEs and on encouraging a broader entrepreneurial spirit. Since then, the share of the trade and services sectors has increased greatly (Hardy and Séguin 2008). Large businesses have largely given way to smaller ones: in 2017, 95.3% of the region's businesses had 1–49 employees compared to 4.7% with more than 50 (including 4.3% with 50–249 employees)[6].

These changes have left important marks in the socio-economic landscape of the territory. Today, the Mauricie region is facing various challenges, particularly in terms of demographics, work and precariousness. In terms of demographics, there has been little population growth over the last 10 years. The region does not seem to be attractive to young people, who often leave after their studies, which leads to an imbalance in the age groups, making the Mauricie one of the regions with the highest demographic dependency ratio[7] in the province. The closure of large factories in the region (as mentioned above) has had an impact on the hiring capacity of these large employers and their subcontractors, creating a relatively high unemployment rate.

All of these factors and their evolution have contributed to the particular situation of precariousness in Mauricie today: the population is relatively poorer and more dependent on government transfers than the provincial

---

6 Portrait économique des régions du Québec, 2018 edition: https://www.economie.gouv.qc.ca/fileadmin/content/documents_support/regions/regional_portraits/socio_econo_portrait.pdf (accessed March 27, 2023).

7 The demographic dependency ratio seeks to demonstrate the demographic burden carried by the working-age population within a certain region. It does this by counting the number of "dependent" people (between 0 and 19 years old and 65 and over) per 100 people of working age.

average. In terms of education, however, real progress has been made: the graduation rate of workers has increased, as has the proportion of those who have attained a post-secondary professional or college-level education. However, the most highly educated individuals still struggle in finding employment in their field of expertise in the region.

In sum, today, the Mauricie region has an increasingly well-educated population but it is struggling to retain its young graduates, who find it difficult to find employment opportunities in the region, and it has a population that is both aging and becoming increasingly impoverished. In response to the closure of large manufacturing companies, the region is increasingly turning to SMEs and entrepreneurial succession to boost the regional economy. However, entrepreneurial succession encounters difficulties, among other things, due to a lack of training in business start-up and because of difficulties in meeting the standard criteria for financing from conventional donors. These are the main challenges identified during the government of Quebec's consultations for the region relating to the Quebec research and innovation strategy: despite the fact that the region is trying to shift towards SMEs and to stimulate innovation among entrepreneurs, it has little latitude and comes up against the rigidity of government support programs and their administrative burden[8].

Fonds Mauricie specifically targets the next generation of entrepreneurs with its support and mentoring services. The mission of Fonds Mauricie is to "develop the economic and human potential of the community by providing access to credit, technical support and sustained mentoring for individuals with viable business projects who have little or no access to traditional financial services"[9]. Founded in 1999, the organization offers mentoring, financing and training services throughout the region. We are interested in the practices of this organization, its role in the entrepreneurial ecosystem and the concrete results obtained in terms of socio-economic development. The data for the impacts are those provided by the organization over a five-year period from 2013 to 2018.

---

[8] Ministère de l'Économie et de l'Innovation du Québec, Mauricie and Centre-du-Québec consultations, stratégie québécoise de la recherche et de l'innovation 2017–2022; highlights from October 7, 2016.

[9] See: https://www.fondsmauricie.com/fr/ (accessed September 24, 2021).

8.2.2. *Proximity support and the creation and maintenance of businesses and jobs*

The practice at the heart of the Fonds Mauricie model is proximity support, which takes the form of technical support adapted to the needs of each entrepreneurial "project promoter" who comes to them. The support can be technical and/or financial, meaning that it can be offered with or without financial support. One third of the projects only receive technical support from advisors. The majority require technical support in addition to a loan, the average amount of which is CAD 7,000. Moreover, the organization diversifies its impact on the entrepreneurial landscape of the region by not only seeking to support new entrepreneurs but also existing businesses to keep them in operation[10]: half of Fonds Mauricie's proximity support work concerns the maintenance of already existing businesses and the other the creation of new businesses. The organization of proximity support is divided into six steps.

The first step is onboarding to verify that the support provided by the organization meets the promoter's needs and to determine the type of support (with or without a loan) that would be appropriate. This meeting can take place individually or in small groups. Then, for the loan program, the promoter is supported in preparing their business plan, which must be submitted to the loan committee. For those who have obtained a loan, this step is followed by the individual follow-up, which goes on until the consolidation of the business. For those without a loan, the support is offered in the same way until the consolidation of the business. The organization also offers training for different aspects of entrepreneurship to the participants, irrespective of whether they have been granted a loan. One advisor expressed Fonds Mauricie's vision with regard to the development of entrepreneurial skills, a vision that places this factor above the criterion of the project's financial set-up:

> At Fonds Mauricie, we don't check first if you have the money, we check if you have the skills, and if you don't, we look to see what can be done to fix this and develop them.

---

10 We mean the action of creating a new company from scratch by a promoter supported within the organization. Conversely, a maintained business means a business that is able to maintain its activity thanks to the technical and/or financial support of the group, but which was therefore already in existence at the time of the initiation of this support from the organization.

Over the five years studied, from 2013 to 2018, a total of 9,756 hours of support and training were provided by Fonds Mauricie to the region's entrepreneurial project holders. We observed that, in terms of the number of hours of support received per project, the training and individual support leading up to the loan are the most important steps. However, in terms of the number of people reached, it is the individual support without a loan that benefitted the greatest number of promoters (525 projects over five years). On average, promoters received 17 hours of training and 9.66 hours of follow-up after a loan was granted. As for the distribution of the support according to the type of project, two thirds of the support included a loan.

We observed that proximity support offered without a loan was used more to maintain businesses than to create them. If we consider the impact results since the organization's founding in 1999, 266 businesses and 676 jobs have been created or maintained. On average, over the five years studied, Fonds Mauricie created or maintained a little more than 16 businesses per year thanks to its proximity support measures (Table 8.2).

Number of companies	2013/2014	2014/2015	2015/2016	2016/2017	2017/2018	Total	%
Created	4	8	11	8	11	42	50
Maintained	13	11	3	12	3	42	50
Total	17	19	14	20	14	84	100

Table 8.2. *Small business creation and maintenance by year with and without a Fonds Mauricie loan from 2013 to 2018*

The businesses created and maintained by Fonds Mauricie are microbusinesses, which create an average of two jobs (Table 8.3). We note that the businesses supported by Fonds Mauricie create or maintain between 30 and 40 jobs per year.

Number of jobs	2013/2014	2014/2015	2015/2016	2016/2017	2017/2018	Total	%
Created	11	12	25	9	22	79	44
Maintained	26	28	5	25	16	100	56
Total	37	40	30	34	38	179	100

Table 8.3. *Job creation and maintenance in businesses supported by Fonds Mauricie from 2013 to 2018*

The businesses supported by Fonds Mauricie are active in various sectors, particularly in the service, arts and culture, restaurant and retail sectors. The average loan granted during the 2013–2018 period varied between CAD 7,254 and 9,013. The repayment rate is around 90%, and the business survival rate after five years is 54%. This is significantly higher than the average business survival rate in Quebec, which is 42%. The sustainable nature of the projects supported by Fonds Mauricie can be explained in part by the quality of the personalized support and by the vision of the organization, which solely devotes itself to viable business projects.

8.2.3. *Factors of social inclusion: atypical entrepreneurs*

Fonds Mauricie's action benefits the region's economic development by supporting people who are on the fringes of traditional financing channels. These people most often have an atypical profile or have original projects that do not fit into the rigid financial frameworks of banking institutions. It is thanks to its approach centered on the individual and their immediate environment that Fonds Mauricie manages to support the emergence of these unconventional entrepreneurs while responding to certain economic and social issues facing the region. This is evident when we analyze the profile of the entrepreneurs who have received support. The main source of income for participants when they came to Fonds Mauricie was income from self-employment (29%), last-resort financial assistance (18%) or a full-time worker's salary (14%).

In total, just over one third of participants were in a precarious economic situation, reporting that they were living primarily on government allowances or had no income (37%), with about half of them living on incomes below the poverty line. Certain segments of the population, particularly young people, older people and people with an immigrant background, are becoming increasingly important to the organization's clients. These groups present demographic challenges for the Mauricie region: the aging of a population that is less and less affluent, the lack of succession in employment and the problem of retaining workers and young people. The analysis of Fonds Mauricie's data for the 2013–2018 period shows that the organization contributes to the inclusion of these specific categories of people in the entrepreneurial dynamics.

The number of women participating in Fonds Mauricie's activities has always been lower than the number of men, at least over the five years studied. On average, there are 66 women for every 100 men, or 39% of the entrepreneurs are women. It is noted that the organization does not reach the parity zone in its clientele. However, if we project these results onto the national statistics for small businesses with one to four employees, we note that the organization integrates a greater proportion of women entrepreneurs in its services compared to the average of 27% in Quebec in 2018[11].

Each year, the organization provides support to a growing number of participants with immigrant backgrounds: in 2018 and 2019, this demographic made up nearly 15% of the people reached (14.1% and 13.7%) compared to 6.4% in 2013–2014, when this statistic began to be recorded. To put this into perspective, note that the immigration rate is 2.4% in Mauricie. Although it is one of the regions of Quebec that welcomes a modest number of immigrants, the need for entrepreneurial support is just as important for these people and their proportion in the organization's clientele is five times higher than the immigration rate in the territory. With the training in entrepreneurship and the proximity support it provides to this clientele, Fonds Mauricie therefore acts as a driver of integration for individuals from immigrant backgrounds who wish to be initiated into the workings of entrepreneurship and pursue their business project in their new host region but frequently lack the resources to qualify with financial institutions and/or need to be guided through the entrepreneurial ecosystem and governmental and municipal bureaucracy.

Finally, with respect to the age profile of its clientele, Fonds Mauricie data indicate that the organization supports small business promoters who are younger than average. This trend is highlighted by the organization's professionals, who also link these dynamics to the profile of promoters calling on their services in terms of education. Most of the participants in Fonds Mauricie had continued their studies beyond high school when they joined the organization. These data are similar to Canadian trends vis-à-vis the level of education of promoters of businesses with one to four employees, with 68% of managers having a post-secondary education, 24%

---

11 Ministère de l'Économie et de l'Innovation du Québec, 2019, portrait de l'entrepreneuriat au Quebec.

having a high school education and 7% not having completed high school[12]. The profile of Fonds Mauricie's clientele is therefore very similar to Canadian trends (Figure 8.1). However, the previous training of project holders who come to Fonds Mauricie is most often in fields far removed from the business world.

It is in this sense that the profile of the organization's clientele is unconventional and that we can understand its role in supporting the inclusion of people who are educated but nevertheless on the fringes of participation in the economic life of their community. This is illustrated by the organization's data and also by those in charge of Fonds Mauricie, who underline the importance of highly educated young people in their client base in recent years. These young people struggle to find professional opportunities in their field of training and face great difficulties in securing finances for their entrepreneurial projects, among other reasons due to lack of personal investment. It is becoming increasingly common for these people to knock on the door of Fonds Mauricie to get the boost they need to start their business.

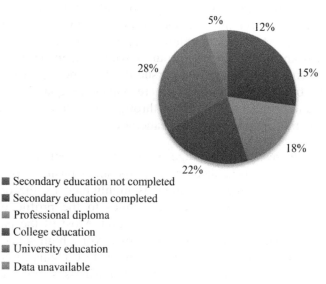

■ Secondary education not completed
■ Secondary education completed
■ Professional diploma
■ College education
■ University education
■ Data unavailable

Figure 8.1. *Typical education level of people applying for Fonds Mauricie support between 2013 and 2018. For a color version of this figure, see www.iste.co.uk/brasseur/inclusive2.zip*

---

12 Statistiques Canada, enquête sur le financement et la croissance des petites et moyennes entreprises 2017.

8.2.4. The entrepreneurial ecosystem: diversification and networking

Fonds Mauricie also plays an important role in the entrepreneurial ecosystem of the territory by promoting the diversification of the SME landscape and encouraging the networking of promoters with each other and with local socio-economic resources. These practices promote the diversification of the entrepreneurial landscape by, among other things, supporting alternative forms of organization. More than the for-profit business model, Fonds Mauricie also seeks to support cooperative entrepreneurship and non-profit organizations (NPOs) in the region by granting bridge loans to NPOs or existing cooperatives or by supporting entrepreneurs in the start-up of not-for-profit projects. The study of the types of legal incorporations chosen by the entrepreneurs receiving support from Fonds Mauricie shows that, although the most popular forms are registration as a self-employed worker and incorporation as a company, many entrepreneurs choose alternative forms of organization in order to make their project a reality. During the 2013–2018 period, there were 4 cooperative incorporations, 13 NPOs and 6 collectives, representing nearly a quarter of the projects supported.

Diversification is also encouraged by a vision of openness towards people with atypical profiles, as well as towards projects that deviate from the norm. This vision of openness is all the more important because in Quebec, as the professionals and administrators of Fonds Mauricie have strongly pointed out, public and parapublic support programs for entrepreneurs have been largely formatted and even sanitized. The tightening of lending policies among the institutional lenders also leaves out a whole series of potential entrepreneurs, such as farmers whose projects are blocked due to the temporal constraints of production, which is also the case for other people whose entrepreneurial rhythm is affected by the seasonal nature of their commercial activity.

Some sectors are excluded almost de facto because of the risk analysis criteria of financial institutions. As one advisor explains, "[y]ou have to have an extremely well put together file, everything has to be perfectly framed. You have to present the right figures, the right profile, otherwise, you can't go through the institutions. Forget about your project!" The absence of limits, brakes or initial restrictions on the type of projects and promoters that can be financed seems to us to be part of the added value of Fonds Mauricie, which thus contributes to the diversification of the economic landscape of the territory it serves. One advisor summed up the organization's philosophy as follows: "We are a land of exceptions!"

> – SIT Mauricie: social economy enterprise for the socio-professional integration of people with mental health problems. Three economic components: subcontracting, recovery and recycling and a stained-glass workshop.
>
> – Le 507: a collective entrepreneurship project that offers a creative space for emerging artists, a boutique, a café and a multipurpose room.
>
> – Citron Rose: a retailer that offers sporty, active and casual clothing for women in sizes 14–26.
>
> – Retouches BVC: a business offering upholstery, covering, repair and adaptation services for furniture.
>
> – Coop Gym: a collective enterprise whose objective is to offer a place for training to the workers of downtown Trois-Rivières.
>
> – Ferme ABC Mékinac: varied production of vegetables, fruits, mushrooms and other farm products.
>
> – Recycle-3R-Mauricie: hiring of and maintaining employment for poor and marginalized people for the development of the recovery and recycling sector in the telecommunications field.
>
> – Karaté sportif: company with a development program through which children learn self-defense, emotional control and conflict management.

Box 8.1. *Businesses recently created with the help of Fonds Mauricie*

Another facet to highlight is the role of Fonds Mauricie as a link in the entrepreneurial ecosystem, particularly in the city of Trois-Rivières, the economic center of the Mauricie region. The organization acts as a driver of social inclusion and economic development for its promoters by connecting them to the rest of the local economic and entrepreneurial environment. An administrator of the organization explains this dynamic:

> Here we are in the search for solutions, in networking. As soon as we need a product or a service, we'll always favor people

who have been through our programs at Fonds Mauricie. If we have the slightest opportunity to promote businesses, we quickly direct it to those who need a little help [...]. It's a very integrated way of working.

The organization sees its role in territorial development as a complement to the limitations of each of the economic development partners when they are unable to support specific promoters. Previously, Fonds Mauricie was forced to knock on the doors of various training and socio-economic support institutions in order to solicit referrals and find new projects to support. Following the evolution of its reputation and credibility in the milieu, the dynamic has been reversed in recent years. The organization no longer has to "chase after anyone" and is instead referred numerous files and projects from promoters who are unable to get support from other entrepreneurial support structures. Explaining the complementary yet essential role of the organization in guaranteeing the inclusiveness of the entrepreneurial ecosystem, one of the advisors illustrated the organization's position as follows: "We are like a molecule that binds the entire economic development universe."

One factor reinforces this role as a link played by Fonds Mauricie. It is the organization's ability to act as a "spark plug" for projects that start up in its wake. The quality of the support offered by the organization strengthens the entrepreneurial projects. In addition, the reputation of the organization sends a signal to potential investors and helps propel many projects forward. This contribution is measurable by the leverage effect indicator generated by the financing of projects; that is, the amounts that the promoters have managed to accumulate with the financial support of the organization. This leverage can be quantified by comparing the amount of loans granted and the total cost of the projects financed.

At Fonds Mauricie, the average leverage was 966% over the 2013–2018 period or a little more than nine times the value of the honorary loan granted by the organization. Fonds Mauricie has become a link in a financial package where other granting organizations can be added, in particular institutions that are more reluctant to finance unusual projects or promoters with an atypical profile and who are waiting for the support from an initial organization, or a local organization, before authorizing subsequent financing. There is also the assurance that the promoter will receive close support, which may lead a subventionary organization to invest in a less conventional project. Fonds Mauricie thus allows access to other financing opportunities that would have been difficult to access without this initial support from community credit.

8.2.5. *The community's contribution to the community*

Fonds Mauricie's mission is also to promote socially responsible investment and community involvement. The organization achieves this by setting up a capitalization fund for honorary loans for promoters from capital originating from the Mauricie region and from interest on investments originating exclusively from socially responsible funds. This ensures the promotion of a model where it is the "community that lends to the community" and where the social and local capital of the organization is enhanced. As of March 31, 2020, the total market capitalization of Fonds Mauricie was CAD 461,806[13]. Apart from two socially responsible investment funds located in Montreal and Toronto, other sources of funding for its venture capital fund are NPOs (such as unions, religious communities, foundations, etc.), institutions and businesses, all from across the Mauricie region.

It should be noted that most of the investments are made with a zero interest rate, which testifies to the organization's deep roots and proximity to its local community and partners, who are aware of Fond Mauricie's mission. The organization thus succeeds in connecting the next generation of entrepreneurs to the environment through its financial partners in the local community. While many NPOs contribute to Fond Mauricie's mission because "they have already integrated this notion of the importance of social and community issues, and the impact it has on the community", private companies and other local economic actors also find value in the organization's economic development activities. As the Director of Fonds Mauricie explains, this model benefits everyone in a community that is facing significant socio-economic challenges: "Businesses already in operation have an interest in supporting the emergence of potential business partners, and that is one of the reasons why they contribute to the organization's activities."

---

13 MicroEntreprendre, annual report 2018–2019, Montreal. Available at: https://microentreprendre.ca/wp-content/uploads/2022/09/RA_2018_2019_MTL.pdf (accessed on March 27, 2023).

Thus, the community lends to the community and also for the community, with a view to both supporting the social inclusion of atypical entrepreneurs, as well as promoting economic development on a local scale.

8.3. Conclusion

Community credit in Quebec brings together actors who have developed an original and innovative approach to socio-economic development that opens the door of entrepreneurship to people who are involved in viable projects but who encounter difficulties in starting and maintaining their activity. The uniqueness of this model compared to the dominant practices of microfinance in developing countries is based on appropriate proximity support and on the local capitalization of funds, which link each of the organizations to the development dynamics of the territories. Territorial anchoring also makes the model unique: each of these organizations operates within a support ecosystem that is rooted in civil society. The uniqueness of this approach creates inclusive dynamics and generates positive impacts "on people's lives, but also on the local community by creating solidarity and partnerships" (management of Fonds Mauricie). Practitioners also believe that they act in response to local and regional devitalization, creating businesses that survive and thus helping to stabilize certain economies.

The case study of Fonds Mauricie sheds light on the contribution of community credit practices to social innovation in territories in two ways. On the one hand, we note the remedial capacities of the entrepreneurial support system that make it more accessible to people on the margins of traditional financial networks. On the other hand, community credit supports entrepreneurship as a means of social integration. In the words of an experienced advisor at Fonds Mauricie, it is a matter of "injecting social helium into the community". By providing support to these people and developing their skills, the groups are practicing a form of support for a "societal start-up". In this sense, it is a form of social innovation that transforms the dynamics of exclusion and disadvantage in the territories. It is from this point of view that the contribution of community credit to inclusion processes appears to hold the most promise.

8.4. References

Guérin, I., Labie, M., Servet, J.M. (2015). *The Crises of Microcredit*. Zed Books, London.

Hamel, P. and Klein, J.L. (1996). Le développement régional au Québec : enjeu de pouvoir et discours politique. In *Le phénomène régional au Québec*, Proulx, M. (ed.). Presses de l'Université du Québec, Quebec.

Hardy, R. and Séguin, N. (2008). *La Mauricie*. Presses de l'Université Laval, Quebec.

Klein, K.J. and Harrison, D.A. (2007). On the diversity of diversity: Tidy logic, messier realities. *Academy of Management Perspectives*, 32(4), 26–34.

Klein, J.L., Camus, A., Jetté, C., Champagne, C., Roy, M. (2016). *La transformation sociale par l'innovation sociale*. Presses de l'Université du Québec, Quebec.

Lamontagne, F. (2000). *Le crédit communautaire : un outil essentiel de développement économique et social*. Réseau québécois du crédit communautaire, Montreal.

Langevin, M. (2013). La mise en forme de l'inclusion financière périphérique. Réactivité et créativité de la microfinance dans son rapport aux crises. *Cahiers de recherche sociologique*, 53, 91–115.

Langevin, M. (2017). L'agencement entre la haute finance et l'univers du développement : des conséquences multiples pour la formation des marchés (micro)financiers. *Canadian Journal of Development Studies/Revue canadienne d'études du développement*, 38(4), 487–506.

Langevin, M. and Jacob, S. (2008). Le crédit communautaire dans la région de la Capitale nationale : conceptualisation, dimensions d'évaluation, impacts et indicateurs. *Cahiers du CRIDÉS*, 8(4).

Lévesques, B. (2014). Un monde qui se défait, un monde à reconstruire. In *L'innovation sociale : les marches d'une construction théorique et pratique*, Lévesques, B., Fontan, J.-M., Klein, J.-L. (eds). Presses de l'Université du Québec, Quebec.

MicroEntreprendre (2019). Annual report 2018–2019 [Online]. Available at: https://microentreprendre.ca/wp-content/uploads/2022/09/RA_2018_2019_MTL.pdf [Accessed March 27, 2023].

Mulgan, G. (2006). The process of social innovation. *Innovations: Technology, Governance, Globalization*, 1(2), 145–162.

Noiseux, Y. (2012). Le travail atypique au Québec : les jeunes au cœur de la dynamique de précarisation par la centrifugation de l'emploi. *Revue multidisciplinaire sur l'emploi*, 7(1), 28–54.

Tremblay, S., Ndjambou, P., Giroux, C., Carrier-Giasson, N. (2017). Le crédit communautaire et la création de microentreprises au Saguenay-Lac-Saint-Jean comme outil de développement économique communautaire et de développement social. Report, GRIR\UQAC, Chicoutimi.

Tremblay, S., Langevin, M., Alberio, M. (2021). La trajectoire du crédit communautaire au Québec : innovation, résistance et recomposition. *6e Colloque international du CRISES. Au carrefour des possibles. Quelles innovations sociales contre les injustices sociales, environnementales et épistémiques ?*, Université du Québec, Quebec.

Conclusion

The Enterprise of Territorial Inclusion: A Societal Transformation

In this book, the development of territorial inclusion is shown to be a "necessary collective project":

– it is "necessary" given the persistence of exclusion phenomena;

– it requires a "collective" approach, since the good will and investment of each actor in a territory will remain ineffective if not combined with local partnerships;

– it is a "project" since inclusion is "something to work towards". Inclusion is never fully realized or finalized and remains a utopia – not in the sense of it being unrealistic, but rather it is an ideal for guiding action and something to always strive towards.

The initiatives taken and the actions carried out are no less concrete and efficient, like the "territories with zero long-term unemployment" experiment, of which two chapters of this volume give accounts from different analytical angles (Chapters 2 and 7). Whether it be, among other situations, two SMEs in Seine-Saint-Denis (Chapter 1) or the Quebec community credit organizations (Chapter 8), the enterprise of inclusion takes the form of a challenge to be met in order to "repair" society, correct inequalities and restore social justice. It starts from three observations: recognizing the possibility of action in a given territory (*I can intervene*), the absence or ineffectiveness of other mechanisms (*if I don't act, nothing will happen*) and the fact that in this context indifference is untenable (*it concerns me*).

Conclusion written by Martine BRASSEUR.

As sociologist Alain Policar points out in an article in *Le Monde:* "Social justice requires, in reality, that which depends on the context and not on choices to be compensated[1]."

It is this compensation that those whom circumstances have endowed them with greater capability, in the sense given by Sen, undertake to make effective. Indeed,

> when addressing the problem of poverty in wealthy countries, one must take into account that many of the 'poor', in terms of income and other primary goods, also have characteristics – age, disability, poor health, etc. – that make it harder for them to convert primary goods into basic capabilities, such as the ability to move about, to lead a healthy life, and to participate in the community (Sen 2002, p. 221).

If these inequalities of circumstance appear as inescapable and linked to the human condition, they are also the result of phenomena produced by society itself and a function of the dominant norms in a given context. This social exclusion "sets aside an individual or group of individuals who present differences or deficiencies judged to be invalidating. Social exclusion puts an individual 'out of the game', excluding them from the game of social relations"[2]. Thus, the compensation undertaken by socio-economic actors in a given territory is also a refusal to reject difference or a certain form of deviance.

Inclusion, insofar as it aims to restore or uphold equality and combat discrimination, requires the recognition of differences. However, the principle of inclusion could paradoxically justify a shift towards communitarianism or towards an injunction to assimilate and conform to society. The project to develop inclusive territories is the opposite of such a conception. Rather, directly linked to diversity, it is a quest for universalism; it is not about the nature of the Other or its appearance – which would be its negation – but a universalism of the relationship with the Other, of otherness, presuming to consider others as other.

---

1 Policar, A. (2021). Le mot "woke" a été transformé en instrument d'occultation des discriminations raciales. *Le Monde*, December 30, 24.
2 Chasseriaud, C. (1992–1993). Grande exclusion sociale. Direction des Affaires Sociales [Online]. Available at: https://francearchives.fr/facomponent/9d03f791d8379695-2946100af 9945699f381a32.

Moreover, what is being undertaken does not only respond to an urgent need to allow everyone to live in decent conditions. It is also the implementation of a humanism that Sartre (2007) linked to existentialism, affirming that every human being must be able to choose themself and that in this possibility of choice what establishes our humanity is defined: "When we say that man chooses himself, not only do we mean that each one of us must choose himself, but also that in choosing himself, he is choosing for all men" (Sartre 2007, p. 31).

The growth of research on inclusion is not a recent phenomenon: it has involved a wide range of scientific disciplines, and numerous works have been published, notably in France by the sociologist Serge Paugam (1996, 2000), over several decades in order to shed light on the causes of exclusion and how we can better remedy it. With the aim of "understanding and acting", social psychologists have also shown how social representations can become tools "in the service of insertion and prevention" beyond stereotyping (Abric 1996, p. 8). In contrast, by approaching the enterprise of inclusion in a territory from the angle of local partnerships, this book, in line with the first volume (which was also compiled with Annie Bartoli, Didier Chabaud, Pascal Grouiez and Gilles Rouet (Brasseur et al. 2023)), highlights the societal transformation that is currently taking place through the evolution of the place of and role incumbent on the enterprise.

Until the end of the 20th century, the problem of exclusion and inclusive practices was the exclusive domain of social workers, and the workplace was only considered in terms of economic concerns (Chevreuse 1979; Chasseriaud 2013). While the institutional emergence of the social and solidarity economy (SSE) is generally located in the 19th century, with a resurgence in the 1970s–1980s (Gianfaldoni 2004), the SSE remained, and still remains, the prerogative of specific organizational forms: difference remained on the margins in a parallel inclusion. Since the beginning of the 21st century, a mutation can be observed, progressively bringing the enterprise to the heart of societal pre-occupations and conferring on it a social utility that finds its full measure in the local partnerships developed within inclusive territories.

In *Entrepreneuriat et insertion* (Brasseur 2010), we had already reported on the obsolescence of the opposition between the two paradigms of the economic and the social. The social purpose of entrepreneurship, which has become both a driver and a practice of integration, was indeed apparent from the various research studies presented and from feedback. The societal role of the enterprise was no longer ignored and the figure of the entrepreneur (who comes from a privileged background in accordance with the dominant profile) was undergoing a transformation.

People who faced exclusion because of a lack of skills became entrepreneurs and changed their relationship of dependence on society. Contributors and no longer recipients of assistance, bearers of innovation and wealth, they changed their relationship to their differences from *toleration* – if we refer to the distinction defined by Crick (1971), considering them as obstacles to professional activity and constraints for management – to a *tolerance* that approaches them as resources and attributes value to them.

This book shows that a new stage has been reached. It is accompanied by other organizational changes, such as the development of democratic practices (Detchessahar 2019). Inclusion is thus becoming the business of companies that are involved in the development of local partnerships in a territory. Managing can no longer be reduced to that which, for philosophers, is the hallmark of the senseless (Spector 2016), i.e. the search for economic profit without concern for common rules. Indeed, the insensible are those who either develop a rhetoric of social injustice which they consider inevitable and irreducible or the "stowaway, free rider, and this within the system itself […] the one who does not contribute to the extent of what they benefit" (Spector 2016, p. 15). The fool only serves their own selfish interests without concern for others and society.

Until recently, the persistence of exclusion found a form of legitimization in a posture of insanity asserted as inherent in the managerial imperatives of companies. However, in the enterprise of territorial inclusion, it is the interdependence of concern for the self and concern for the other that is affirmed as the interrelation between both social justice and individual interests. As Foucault (2013, p. 91) pointed out in 1980 in a conference on the origin of the hermeneutics of the self, "we must promote new forms of subjectivity by refusing the type of individuality that has been imposed on us for several centuries". It is this enterprise that is the work, bringing about the emergence of a society of care on a territory and transforming the social roles of the entrepreneur and the manager.

This book shows that not only is the unthought no longer appropriate but that the ridiculous has had its day. It is only the beginning of a strand of research and practices that can be built on and furthered.

References

Abric, J.C. (ed.) (1996). *Exclusion sociale, insertion et prévention*. Erès, Saint-Agne.

Brasseur, M. (ed.) (2010). *Entrepreneuriat et insertion*. Bruylant, Brussels.

Brasseur, M., Bartoli, A., Chabaud, D., Grouiez, P., Rouet, G. (2023). *Inclusive Territories 1: Role of Businesses and Organizations*. ISTE Ltd, London, and John Wiley & Sons, New York.

Chasseriaud, C. (2013). Société et travail social. *La revue française de service social*, 251, 20–31.

Chevreuse, C. (1979). *Pratiques inventives du travail social*. Les Éditions ouvrières, Paris.

Crick, B. (1971). Toleration and tolerance in theory and practice. *Government and Opposition*, 6(2), 143–171.

Detchessahar, M. (ed.) (2019). *L'entreprise délibérée. Refonder le management par le dialogue*. Nouvelle Cité, Paris.

Foucault, M. (2013). *L'origine de l'herméneutique de soi. Conférences prononcées à Dartmouth College, 1980*. Vrin, Paris.

Gianfaldoni, P. (2004). Utilité sociale versus utilité économique. L'entrepreneuriat en économie solidaire. *Écologie et politique*, 28, 93–103.

Paugam, S. (ed.) (1996). *L'exclusion, l'état des savoirs*. La Découverte, Paris.

Paugam, S. (2000). *La disqualification sociale*. PUF, Paris.

Sartre, J.P. (2007). *Existentialism Is a Humanism*. Yale University Press, New Haven.

Sen, A. (2002). *Éthique et économies et autres essais*. PUF, Paris.

Spector, C. (2016). *Éloges de l'injustice. La philosophie face à la déraison*. Le Seuil, Paris.

List of Authors

Annie BARTOLI
LAREQUOI
Paris-Saclay University
Versailles
France

Martine BRASSEUR
CEDAG
Paris Cité University
France

Nathalie CARIOU GHANTOUS
Saint-Joseph University
Beirut
Lebanon

Didier CHABAUD
Chaire ETI
IAE Paris Sorbonne
France

Jean-François CHANLAT
DRM
Paris Dauphine University
France

Mathilde CHOMLAFEL
CRDT
University of Reims
Champagne-Ardenne
France

Laurence FROLOFF BROUCHE
IGE
Saint-Joseph University
Beirut
Lebanon

Pascal GROUIEZ
LADYSS
Paris Cité University
France

Hacène LAÏCHOUR
DRM
Paris Dauphine University
France

Marie LANGEVIN
ESG UQAM
Université du Québec
Montreal
Canada

Jean-Paul MÉREAUX
CRDT
University of Reims
Champagne-Ardenne
France

Amélie NOTAIS
ARGUMANS
Le Mans University
France

Jean-Marie PERETTI
QDM
ESSEC Business School
Cergy
France

Gilles ROUET
LAREQUOI
ISM/IAE Versailles
Saint-Quentin-en-Yvelines
Paris-Saclay University
France

Jean-Christophe SARROT
ATD Fourth World France
Montreuil
France

Amina SAYDI
CEDAG
Paris Cité University
France

Julie TIXIER
IRG
Gustave Eiffel University
Champs-sur-Marne
France

Annie-Claude VEILLEUX
CIRADD
Carleton-sur-Mer
Canada

Index

C, D

capabilities, 57, 58, 61, 63, 64, 68, 69
community credit, 145–148, 151, 162, 163
CSR (corporate social responsibility) (*see also* ethics *and* social responsibility), 4, 5, 76, 89, 90
development
　economic, 64, 137, 147–150, 156, 160–163
　social, 145, 151
　territorial, 146, 151, 161
discriminated populations, 1
discrimination, 4, 7, 9, 12, 48, 50, 82, 90, 98
diversity
　and inclusion, 3, 76, 90–93, 96
　management, 4, 5
dynamics
　entrepreneurial (*see also* entrepreneurship), 156
　inclusive partnership, 127

E

ecosystems, 73, 150
　entrepreneurial, 73

employment/job, 3, 5, 7–9, 11, 13, 22, 31–33, 35, 43, 48–50, 59, 61, 77, 79, 80, 83, 85, 88, 89, 127–141, 147, 149, 153, 156, 160
enterprise (*see also* SME), 5, 6, 8–17, 21, 23, 24, 31, 33, 42, 43, 45, 48, 49, 61, 62, 64, 65, 88–91, 93, 96, 129, 136, 142, 149, 150, 153, 154, 157–160
　social, 21, 23, 24
entrepreneurship (*see also* entrepreneurial dynamics), 13, 25, 26, 30, 31, 34, 58, 61, 63, 65–70, 147, 149, 154, 157, 159–161, 163
ethics (*see also* CSR *and* social responsibility), 5, 43, 92
exclusion (*see also* inclusion), 22, 35, 43, 52, 75–88, 111, 114, 122, 124, 128, 132, 141, 163
　fighting, 75, 76, 78, 80, 81, 83–90, 97, 100

G, H, I

gender, 46, 48, 90, 91, 96
governance, 24, 97, 105–107, 112, 114, 115, 118, 120, 121, 123, 134, 139

human capital, 26
inclusion (*see also* exclusion), 1, 3, 4, 14, 16, 17, 21–24, 28, 30, 35, 41, 52, 57–61, 64, 68, 69, 75, 76, 79, 80, 84–100, 106, 111–116, 122–124, 131, 142, 145–147, 149, 151, 156, 158, 160, 163
inclusive
　city, 60, 96–98
　practice, 21–23
inequalities, 42, 43, 49, 61, 99, 128, 137, 142
　social, 59
innovation, 29, 93, 95, 146, 153, 157, 163
　social, 146

L, N, O

local partnerships, 142
neo-institutional theory, 21, 24, 26, 28, 30
organization (*see also* enterprise), 4, 7, 10, 16, 21, 23, 26, 28, 65, 89, 90, 100, 106–108, 110–113, 115, 116, 122, 141, 154, 160

P, R, S

poverty, 6, 22, 59, 64, 77, 78, 80, 81, 83–86, 141, 147, 156
public policies, 75, 89, 96, 100, 128, 131, 139, 140

resilience, 41, 42, 44, 50, 51, 53, 129, 149
SME (small- and medium-sized enterprise), 3–6, 14–17, 152, 153, 159
social
　and solidarity economy, 23, 24, 31, 135, 140, 145, 147
　responsibility (*see also* CSR *and* ethics), 4, 44, 76, 89, 91, 96
stakeholders, 73, 75, 106, 114, 115, 123, 139
stigmatization, 41–44, 52, 77, 81

U, V, W

unemployment, 3, 6, 21, 30–32, 36, 79, 82–84, 86, 88, 127–129, 131, 132, 134, 136, 137, 141, 152
　long-term, 21, 31, 32, 36, 86, 127, 128, 130–132, 134, 136, 137, 141
vulnerable people, 145, 148, 149, 151
women, 9, 41, 45, 47, 48, 52, 57, 62–69, 128, 145, 150, 157, 160
　entrepreneurs, 57

Other titles from

in

Innovation, Entrepreneurship and Management

2023

BOUVIER-PATRON Paul
Frugal Innovation and Innovative Creation
(Smart Innovation Set – Volume 40)

BRASSEUR Martine, BARTOLI Annie, CHABAUD Didier, GROUIEZ Pascal, ROUET Gilles
Inclusive Territories 1
(Territorial Entrepreneurship and Innovation Set – Volume 1)

CASADELLA Vanessa, UZUNIDIS Dimitri
Agri-Innovations and Development Challenges: Engineering, Value Chains and Socio-economic Models
(Innovation in Engineering and Technology Set – Volume 8)

DARTIGUEPEYROU Carine, SALOFF-COSTE Michel
Futures: The Great Turn
(Innovation and Technology Set – Volume 18)

PEYROUX Élisabeth, RAIMOND Christine, VIEL Vincent, VALIE Émilie
Development and Territorial Restructuring in an Era of Global Change: Theories, Approaches and Future Research Perspectives

SAULAIS Pierre
Knowledge and Ideation: Inventive Knowledge Analysis for Ideation Stimulation
(Innovation and Technology Set – Volume 17)

2022

AOUINAÏT Camille
Open Innovation Strategies
(Smart Innovation Set – Volume 39)

BOUCHÉ Geneviève
Productive Economy, Contributory Economy: Governance Tools for the Third Millennium
(Innovation and Technology Set – Volume 15)

BRUYÈRE Christelle
Caring Management in Health Organizations: A Lever for Crisis Management
(Health and Innovation Set – Volume 3)

HELLER David
Valuation of the Liability Structure by Real Options
(Modern Finance, Management Innovation and Economic Growth Set – Volume 5)

MATHIEU Valérie
A Customer-oriented Manager for B2B Services: Principles and Implementation

MORALES Lucía, DZEVER Sam, TAYLOR Robert
Asia-Europe Industrial Connectivity in Times of Crisis
(Innovation and Technology Set – Volume 16)

NOËL Florent, SCHMIDT Géraldine
Employability and Industrial Mutations: Between Individual Trajectories and Organizational Strategic Planning
(Technological Changes and Human Resources Set – Volume 4)

DE SAINT JULIEN Odile
The Innovation Ecosystem as a Source of Value Creation: A Value Creation Lever for Open Innovation
(Diverse and Global Perspectives on Value Creation Set – Volume 4)

SALOFF-COSTE Michel
Innovation Ecosystems: The Future of Civilizations and the Civilization of the Future
(Innovation and Technology Set – Volume 14)

VAYRE Emilie
Digitalization of Work: New Spaces and New Working Times
(Technological Changes and Human Resources Set – Volume 5)

ZAFEIRIS Konstantinos N, SKIADIS Christos H, DIMOTIKALIS Yannis, KARAGRIGORIOU Alex, KARAGRIGORIOU-VONTA Christina
Data Analysis and Related Applications 1: Computational, Algorithmic and Applied Economic Data Analysis
(Big Data, Artificial Intelligence and Data Analysis Set – Volume 9)
Data Analysis and Related Applications 2: Multivariate, Health and Demographic Data Analysis
(Big Data, Artificial Intelligence and Data Analysis Set – Volume 10)

2021

ARCADE Jacques
Strategic Engineering
(Innovation and Technology Set – Volume 11)

BÉRANGER Jérôme, RIZOULIÈRES Roland
The Digital Revolution in Health
(Health and Innovation Set – Volume 2)

BOBILLIER CHAUMON Marc-Eric
Digital Transformations in the Challenge of Activity and Work: Understanding and Supporting Technological Changes
(Technological Changes and Human Resources Set – Volume 3)

BUCLET Nicolas
Territorial Ecology and Socio-ecological Transition
(Smart Innovation Set – Volume 34)

DIMOTIKALIS Yannis, KARAGRIGORIOU Alex, PARPOULA Christina, SKIADIS Christos H
Applied Modeling Techniques and Data Analysis 1: Computational Data Analysis Methods and Tools
(Big Data, Artificial Intelligence and Data Analysis Set - Volume 7)
Applied Modeling Techniques and Data Analysis 2: Financial, Demographic, Stochastic and Statistical Models and Methods
(Big Data, Artificial Intelligence and Data Analysis Set – Volume 8)

DISPAS Christophe, KAYANAKIS Georges, SERVEL Nicolas, STRIUKOVA Ludmila
Innovation and Financial Markets
(Innovation between Risk and Reward Set – Volume 7)

ENJOLRAS Manon
Innovation and Export: The Joint Challenge of the Small Company
(Smart Innovation Set – Volume 37)

FLEURY Sylvain, RICHIR Simon
Immersive Technologies to Accelerate Innovation: How Virtual and Augmented Reality Enables the Co-Creation of Concepts
(Smart Innovation Set – Volume 38)

GIORGINI Pierre
The Contributory Revolution
(Innovation and Technology Set – Volume 13)

GOGLIN Christian
Emotions and Values in Equity Crowdfunding Investment Choices 2: Modeling and Empirical Study

GRENIER Corinne, OIRY Ewan
Altering Frontiers: Organizational Innovations in Healthcare
(Health and Innovation Set – Volume 1)

GUERRIER Claudine
Security and Its Challenges in the 21st Century
(Innovation and Technology Set – Volume 12)

HELLER David
Performance of Valuation Methods in Financial Transactions
(Modern Finance, Management Innovation and Economic Growth Set – Volume 4)

LEHMANN Paul-Jacques
Liberalism and Capitalism Today

SOULÉ Bastien, HALLÉ Julie, VIGNAL Bénédicte, BOUTROY Éric, NIER Olivier
Innovation in Sport: Innovation Trajectories and Process Optimization
(Smart Innovation Set – Volume 35)

UZUNIDIS Dimitri, KASMI Fedoua, ADATTO Laurent
Innovation Economics, Engineering and Management Handbook 1: Main Themes
Innovation Economics, Engineering and Management Handbook 2: Special Themes

VALLIER Estelle
Innovation in Clusters: Science–Industry Relationships in the Face of Forced Advancement
(Smart Innovation Set – Volume 36)

2020

ACH Yves-Alain, RMADI-SAÏD Sandra
Financial Information and Brand Value: Reflections, Challenges and Limitations

ANDREOSSO-O'CALLAGHAN Bernadette, DZEVER Sam, JAUSSAUD Jacques, TAYLOR Robert
Sustainable Development and Energy Transition in Europe and Asia
(Innovation and Technology Set – Volume 9)

BEN SLIMANE Sonia, M'HENNI Hatem
Entrepreneurship and Development: Realities and Future Prospects
(Smart Innovation Set – Volume 30)

CHOUTEAU Marianne, FOREST Joëlle, NGUYEN Céline
Innovation for Society: The P.S.I. Approach
(Smart Innovation Set – Volume 28)

CORON Clotilde
Quantifying Human Resources: Uses and Analysis
(Technological Changes and Human Resources Set – Volume 2)

CORON Clotilde, GILBERT Patrick
Technological Change
(Technological Changes and Human Resources Set – Volume 1)

CERDIN Jean-Luc, PERETTI Jean-Marie
The Success of Apprenticeships: Views of Stakeholders on Training and Learning (Human Resources Management Set – Volume 3)

DELCHET-COCHET Karen
Circular Economy: From Waste Reduction to Value Creation
(Economic Growth Set – Volume 2)

DIDAY Edwin, GUAN Rong, SAPORTA Gilbert, WANG Huiwen
Advances in Data Science
(Big Data, Artificial Intelligence and Data Analysis Set – Volume 4)

DOS SANTOS PAULINO Victor
Innovation Trends in the Space Industry
(Smart Innovation Set – Volume 25)

GASMI Nacer
Corporate Innovation Strategies: Corporate Social Responsibility and Shared Value Creation
(Smart Innovation Set – Volume 33)

GOGLIN Christian
Emotions and Values in Equity Crowdfunding Investment Choices 1: Transdisciplinary Theoretical Approach

GUILHON Bernard
Venture Capital and the Financing of Innovation
(Innovation Between Risk and Reward Set – Volume 6)

LATOUCHE Pascal
Open Innovation: Human Set-up
(Innovation and Technology Set – Volume 10)

LIMA Marcos
Entrepreneurship and Innovation Education: Frameworks and Tools
(Smart Innovation Set – Volume 32)

MACHADO Carolina, DAVIM J. Paulo
Sustainable Management for Managers and Engineers

MAKRIDES Andreas, KARAGRIGORIOU Alex, SKIADAS Christos H.
Data Analysis and Applications 3: Computational, Classification, Financial, Statistical and Stochastic Methods
(Big Data, Artificial Intelligence and Data Analysis Set – Volume 5)
Data Analysis and Applications 4: Financial Data Analysis and Methods
(Big Data, Artificial Intelligence and Data Analysis Set – Volume 6)

MASSOTTE Pierre, CORSI Patrick
Complex Decision-Making in Economy and Finance

MEUNIER François-Xavier
Dual Innovation Systems: Concepts, Tools and Methods
(Smart Innovation Set – Volume 31)

MICHAUD Thomas
Science Fiction and Innovation Design
(Innovation in Engineering and Technology Set – Volume 6)

MONINO Jean-Louis
Data Control: Major Challenge for the Digital Society
(Smart Innovation Set – Volume 29)

MORLAT Clément
Sustainable Productive System: Eco-development versus Sustainable Development (Smart Innovation Set – Volume 26)

SAULAIS Pierre, ERMINE Jean-Louis
Knowledge Management in Innovative Companies 2: Understanding and Deploying a KM Plan within a Learning Organization
(Smart Innovation Set – Volume 27)

2019

AMENDOLA Mario, GAFFARD Jean-Luc
Disorder and Public Concern Around Globalization

BARBAROUX Pierre
Disruptive Technology and Defence Innovation Ecosystems
(Innovation in Engineering and Technology Set – Volume 5)

DOU Henri, JUILLET Alain, CLERC Philippe
Strategic Intelligence for the Future 1: A New Strategic and Operational Approach
Strategic Intelligence for the Future 2: A New Information Function Approach

FRIKHA Azza
Measurement in Marketing: Operationalization of Latent Constructs

FRIMOUSSE Soufyane
Innovation and Agility in the Digital Age
(Human Resources Management Set – Volume 2)

GAY Claudine, SZOSTAK Bérangère L.
Innovation and Creativity in SMEs: Challenges, Evolutions and Prospects
(Smart Innovation Set – Volume 21)

GORIA Stéphane, HUMBERT Pierre, ROUSSEL Benoît
Information, Knowledge and Agile Creativity
(Smart Innovation Set – Volume 22)

HELLER David
Investment Decision-making Using Optional Models
(Economic Growth Set – Volume 2)

HELLER David, DE CHADIRAC Sylvain, HALAOUI Lana, JOUVET Camille
The Emergence of Start-ups
(Economic Growth Set – Volume 1)

HÉRAUD Jean-Alain, KERR Fiona, BURGER-HELMCHEN Thierry
Creative Management of Complex Systems
(Smart Innovation Set – Volume 19)

LATOUCHE Pascal
Open Innovation: Corporate Incubator
(Innovation and Technology Set – Volume 7)

LEHMANN Paul-Jacques
The Future of the Euro Currency

LEIGNEL Jean-Louis, MÉNAGER Emmanuel, YABLONSKY Serge
Sustainable Enterprise Performance: A Comprehensive Evaluation Method

LIÈVRE Pascal, AUBRY Monique, GAREL Gilles
Management of Extreme Situations: From Polar Expeditions to Exploration-Oriented Organizations

MILLOT Michel
Embarrassment of Product Choices 2: Towards a Society of Well-being

N'GOALA Gilles, PEZ-PÉRARD Virginie, PRIM-ALLAZ Isabelle
Augmented Customer Strategy: CRM in the Digital Age

NIKOLOVA Blagovesta
The RRI Challenge: Responsibilization in a State of Tension with Market Regulation
(Innovation and Responsibility Set – Volume 3)

PELLEGRIN-BOUCHER Estelle, ROY Pierre
Innovation in the Cultural and Creative Industries
(Innovation and Technology Set – Volume 8)

PRIOLON Joël
Financial Markets for Commodities

QUINIOU Matthieu
Blockchain: The Advent of Disintermediation

RAVIX Joël-Thomas, DESCHAMPS Marc
Innovation and Industrial Policies
(Innovation between Risk and Reward Set – Volume 5)

ROGER Alain, VINOT Didier
Skills Management: New Applications, New Questions
(Human Resources Management Set – Volume 1)

SAULAIS Pierre, ERMINE Jean-Louis
Knowledge Management in Innovative Companies 1: Understanding and Deploying a KM Plan within a Learning Organization
(Smart Innovation Set – Volume 23)

SERVAJEAN-HILST Romaric
Co-innovation Dynamics: The Management of Client-Supplier Interactions for Open Innovation
(Smart Innovation Set – Volume 20)

SKIADAS Christos H., BOZEMAN James R.
Data Analysis and Applications 1: Clustering and Regression, Modeling-estimating, Forecasting and Data Mining
(Big Data, Artificial Intelligence and Data Analysis Set – Volume 2)
Data Analysis and Applications 2: Utilization of Results in Europe and Other Topics
(Big Data, Artificial Intelligence and Data Analysis Set – Volume 3)

UZUNIDIS Dimitri
Systemic Innovation: Entrepreneurial Strategies and Market Dynamics

VIGEZZI Michel
World Industrialization: Shared Inventions, Competitive Innovations and Social Dynamics
(Smart Innovation Set – Volume 24)

2018

BURKHARDT Kirsten
Private Equity Firms: Their Role in the Formation of Strategic Alliances

CALLENS Stéphane
Creative Globalization
(Smart Innovation Set – Volume 16)

CASADELLA Vanessa
Innovation Systems in Emerging Economies: MINT – Mexico, Indonesia, Nigeria, Turkey
(Smart Innovation Set – Volume 18)

CHOUTEAU Marianne, FOREST Joëlle, NGUYEN Céline
Science, Technology and Innovation Culture
(Innovation in Engineering and Technology Set – Volume 3)

CORLOSQUET-HABART Marine, JANSSEN Jacques
Big Data for Insurance Companies
(Big Data, Artificial Intelligence and Data Analysis Set – Volume 1)

CROS Françoise
Innovation and Society
(Smart Innovation Set – Volume 15)

DEBREF Romain
Environmental Innovation and Ecodesign: Certainties and Controversies
(Smart Innovation Set – Volume 17)

DOMINGUEZ Noémie
SME Internationalization Strategies: Innovation to Conquer New Markets

ERMINE Jean-Louis
Knowledge Management: The Creative Loop
(Innovation and Technology Set – Volume 5)

GILBERT Patrick, BOBADILLA Natalia, GASTALDI Lise,
LE BOULAIRE Martine, LELEBINA Olga
Innovation, Research and Development Management

IBRAHIMI Mohammed
Mergers & Acquisitions: Theory, Strategy, Finance

LEMAÎTRE Denis
Training Engineers for Innovation

LÉVY Aldo, BEN BOUHENI Faten, AMMI Chantal
Financial Management: USGAAP and IFRS Standards
(Innovation and Technology Set – Volume 6)

MILLOT Michel
Embarrassment of Product Choices 1: How to Consume Differently

PANSERA Mario, OWEN Richard
Innovation and Development: The Politics at the Bottom of the Pyramid
(Innovation and Responsibility Set – Volume 2)

RICHEZ Yves
Corporate Talent Detection and Development

SACHETTI Philippe, ZUPPINGER Thibaud
New Technologies and Branding
(Innovation and Technology Set – Volume 4)

SAMIER Henri
Intuition, Creativity, Innovation

TEMPLE Ludovic, COMPAORÉ SAWADOGO Eveline M.F.W.
Innovation Processes in Agro-Ecological Transitions in Developing Countries
(Innovation in Engineering and Technology Set – Volume 2)

UZUNIDIS Dimitri
Collective Innovation Processes: Principles and Practices
(Innovation in Engineering and Technology Set – Volume 4)

VAN HOOREBEKE Delphine
The Management of Living Beings or Emo-management

2017

AÏT-EL-HADJ Smaïl
The Ongoing Technological System
(Smart Innovation Set – Volume 11)

BAUDRY Marc, DUMONT Béatrice
Patents: Prompting or Restricting Innovation?
(Smart Innovation Set – Volume 12)

BÉRARD Céline, TEYSSIER Christine
Risk Management: Lever for SME Development and Stakeholder Value Creation

CHALENÇON Ludivine
Location Strategies and Value Creation of International Mergers and Acquisitions

CHAUVEL Danièle, BORZILLO Stefano
The Innovative Company: An Ill-defined Object
(Innovation between Risk and Reward Set – Volume 1)

CORSI Patrick
Going Past Limits To Growth

D'ANDRIA Aude, GABARRET Inés
Building 21st Century Entrepreneurship
(Innovation and Technology Set – Volume 2)

DAIDJ Nabyla
Cooperation, Coopetition and Innovation
(Innovation and Technology Set – Volume 3)

FERNEZ-WALCH Sandrine
The Multiple Facets of Innovation Project Management
(Innovation between Risk and Reward Set – Volume 4)

FOREST Joëlle
Creative Rationality and Innovation
(Smart Innovation Set – Volume 14)

GUILHON Bernard
Innovation and Production Ecosystems
(Innovation between Risk and Reward Set – Volume 2)

HAMMOUDI Abdelhakim, DAIDJ Nabyla
Game Theory Approach to Managerial Strategies and Value Creation
(Diverse and Global Perspectives on Value Creation Set – Volume 3)

LALLEMENT Rémi
Intellectual Property and Innovation Protection: New Practices and New Policy Issues
(Innovation between Risk and Reward Set – Volume 3)

LAPERCHE Blandine
Enterprise Knowledge Capital
(Smart Innovation Set – Volume 13)

LEBERT Didier, EL YOUNSI Hafida
International Specialization Dynamics
(Smart Innovation Set – Volume 9)

MAESSCHALCK Marc
Reflexive Governance for Research and Innovative Knowledge
(Responsible Research and Innovation Set – Volume 6)

MASSOTTE Pierre
Ethics in Social Networking and Business 1: Theory, Practice and Current Recommendations
Ethics in Social Networking and Business 2: The Future and Changing Paradigms

MASSOTTE Pierre, CORSI Patrick
Smart Decisions in Complex Systems

MEDINA Mercedes, HERRERO Mónica, URGELLÉS Alicia
Current and Emerging Issues in the Audiovisual Industry
(Diverse and Global Perspectives on Value Creation Set – Volume 1)

MICHAUD Thomas
Innovation, Between Science and Science Fiction
(Smart Innovation Set – Volume 10)

PELLÉ Sophie
Business, Innovation and Responsibility
(Responsible Research and Innovation Set – Volume 7)

SAVIGNAC Emmanuelle
The Gamification of Work: The Use of Games in the Workplace

SUGAHARA Satoshi, DAIDJ Nabyla, USHIO Sumitaka
*Value Creation in Management Accounting and Strategic Management:
An Integrated Approach*
(Diverse and Global Perspectives on Value Creation Set – Volume 2)

UZUNIDIS Dimitri, SAULAIS Pierre
Innovation Engines: Entrepreneurs and Enterprises in a Turbulent World
(Innovation in Engineering and Technology Set – Volume 1)

2016

BARBAROUX Pierre, ATTOUR Amel, SCHENK Eric
Knowledge Management and Innovation
(Smart Innovation Set – Volume 6)

BEN BOUHENI Faten, AMMI Chantal, LEVY Aldo
*Banking Governance, Performance And Risk-Taking: Conventional Banks
Vs Islamic Banks*

BOUTILLIER Sophie, CARRÉ Denis, LEVRATTO Nadine
Entrepreneurial Ecosystems
(Smart Innovation Set – Volume 2)

BOUTILLIER Sophie, UZUNIDIS Dimitri
The Entrepreneur
(Smart Innovation Set – Volume 8)

BOUVARD Patricia, SUZANNE Hervé
Collective Intelligence Development in Business

GALLAUD Delphine, LAPERCHE Blandine
Circular Economy, Industrial Ecology and Short Supply Chains
(Smart Innovation Set – Volume 4)

GUERRIER Claudine
Security and Privacy in the Digital Era
(Innovation and Technology Set – Volume 1)

MEGHOUAR Hicham
Corporate Takeover Targets

MONINO Jean-Louis, SEDKAOUI Soraya
*Big Data, Open Data and Data Development
(Smart Innovation Set – Volume 3)*

MOREL Laure, LE ROUX Serge
*Fab Labs: Innovative User
(Smart Innovation Set – Volume 5)*

PICARD Fabienne, TANGUY Corinne
*Innovations and Techno-ecological Transition
(Smart Innovation Set – Volume 7)*

2015

CASADELLA Vanessa, LIU Zeting, DIMITRI Uzunidis
*Innovation Capabilities and Economic Development in Open Economies
(Smart Innovation Set – Volume 1)*

CORSI Patrick, MORIN Dominique
Sequencing Apple's DNA

CORSI Patrick, NEAU Erwan
Innovation Capability Maturity Model

FAIVRE-TAVIGNOT Bénédicte
Social Business and Base of the Pyramid

GODÉ Cécile
Team Coordination in Extreme Environments

MAILLARD Pierre
Competitive Quality and Innovation

MASSOTTE Pierre, CORSI Patrick
Operationalizing Sustainability

MASSOTTE Pierre, CORSI Patrick
Sustainability Calling

2014

DUBÉ Jean, LEGROS Diègo
Spatial Econometrics Using Microdata

LESCA Humbert, LESCA Nicolas
Strategic Decisions and Weak Signals

2013

HABART-CORLOSQUET Marine, JANSSEN Jacques, MANCA Raimondo
VaR Methodology for Non-Gaussian Finance

2012

DAL PONT Jean-Pierre
Process Engineering and Industrial Management

MAILLARD Pierre
Competitive Quality Strategies

POMEROL Jean-Charles
Decision-Making and Action

SZYLAR Christian
UCITS Handbook

2011

LESCA Nicolas
Environmental Scanning and Sustainable Development

LESCA Nicolas, LESCA Humbert
Weak Signals for Strategic Intelligence: Anticipation Tool for Managers

MERCIER-LAURENT Eunika
Innovation Ecosystems

2010

SZYLAR Christian
Risk Management under UCITS III/IV

2009

COHEN Corine
Business Intelligence

ZANINETTI Jean-Marc
Sustainable Development in the USA

2008

CORSI Patrick, DULIEU Mike
The Marketing of Technology Intensive Products and Services

DZEVER Sam, JAUSSAUD Jacques, ANDREOSSO Bernadette
Evolving Corporate Structures and Cultures in Asia: Impact of Globalization

2007

AMMI Chantal
Global Consumer Behavior

2006

BOUGHZALA Imed, ERMINE Jean-Louis
Trends in Enterprise Knowledge Management

CORSI Patrick, CHRISTOFOL Hervé, RICHIR Simon, SAMIER Henri
Innovation Engineering: the power of intangible networks

Printed and bound by CPI Group (UK) Ltd, Croydon, CR0 4YY
18/03/2024

14472321-0001